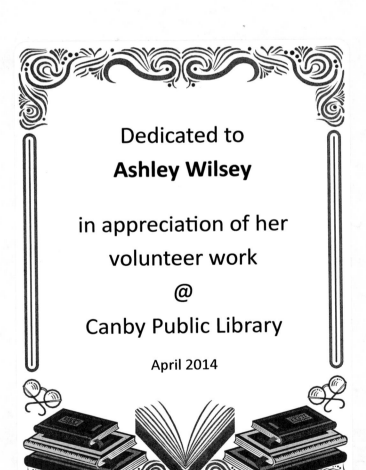

Dedicated to
Ashley Wilsey

in appreciation of her
volunteer work
@
Canby Public Library

April 2014

How to Help Stray Pets and Not Get Stuck
by Diane Carey

ISBN 978-1-938467-98-1

Published by

◤ köehlerbooks ™

210 60th Street
Virginia Beach, VA 23451
212-574-7939
www.koehlerbooks.com

Publisher
John Köehler

Executive Editor
Joe Coccaro

On the cover: Author Diane Carey and Greg Brodeur's three children: Lydia Rose
Frederick, Benjamin Brodeur, and Gordon Brodeur. The pets are all rescued, includ-
ing Gordon's Samoyed, Mozart, and Lydia's chow-shepherd mix, Jackson.
Photo by Ayaz P. Jafri of Owosso, Michigan

iPad photo paintings on back cover and text
by John Koehler, using the *Brushes* app

Also by Diane Carey

CHILDREN'S BOOKS
Buried Alive
Dangerzone
Million Dollar Mistake
Promise You'll Stop
Roughing It
Twist of Fate

HISTORICAL NOVELS
Distant Drums
Rise Defiant
Banners (09/2014)
Do you Have a Beaumont Doctor?

ALIENS SERIES
Cauldron
DNA War

STAR TREK ORIGINAL SERIES
Chainmail Gateways #2
Challenger Newearth #6
Battlestations
Dreadnought
Best Destiny
First Frontier
Final Frontier
Star Trek Invasion - First Strike

STAR TREK THE NEXT GENERATION
Ship of the Line
Ghost Ship

VOYAGER SERIES
Endgame
Captain's Table - Fireship

DEDICATION

This book is dedicated to my husband, Greg
Brodeur, who not only put up with a seemingly
endless stream of unexpected animals,
but who helped care for them selflessly, and to
my children, Lydia, Gordon and Ben, who grew
up with lives often disrupted by stray pets and
their needs, and who grew up to carry on
the family tradition.

HOW TO HELP
STRAY PETS
AND NOT GET STUCK

*One family rescues over 400 dogs, cats,
and the occasional bird, and shares how to do it.*

DIANE CAREY

VIRGINIA BEACH
CAPE CHARLES

AUTHOR'S NOTE

These stories and methods of responsible animal rescue are personal to our family and friends.

They are true, but not necessarily in chronological order. Our methods work, but everything here is meant as friendly advice. We're not professional trainers, a rescue center or a pound. We're more like a halfway house that gives orphaned animals a new start. We're temporary stewards, not adoptive parents. This book isn't for people who go whole-hog into a stray recycling operation (or "re-homing" as it's often called in the trade), conducting laudable but complex and time-consuming adoption services. I give those people my highest respect, but they already know what to do.

How To Help Stray Pets And Not Get Stuck is for those who don't want to or can't make such a commitment. This is for those among you who see a stray pet on the road or in your neighborhood, and feel that hurtful constriction in your chest, that desperation and helplessness, that wish to be able to do something, but you just don't know what to do. This book is a "how-to" manual that prepares you emotionally and physically to be a good samaritan.

This book gives several hints so you can help stray pets without bringing chaos into your life. None are requirements, of course. You may choose to enact some of these ideas and not others. You may use none of them, but just use the book as a message of encouragement and empowerment. I've been careful to include the little spiritual elements brought to me through my years of helping stray pets.

By helping you, our family can help more animals through you. And, in turn, we hope that each of you teaches someone else how to help strays and abandoned pets. We'll continue to do our part, too. Part of the proceeds from the sale of this book will be donated to The Humane Society.

TABLE OF CONTENTS

Little Ben Brodeur, himself adopted from Guatemala, holds the smallest kitten ever rescued by Diane and Greg.

Lesson 1

WELCOME TO COMPASSION

In 1979, my fiancé and I picked up a stray puppy. This little waif was shuffling along the sidewalk in a bad part of town, eating cigarette butts. She was small, something like a Chihuahua mix, though we were never sure. We already had a dog, a large black flat-coated retriever who had been rescued from running free over six months by a neighbor of ours. We were struggling with two low-paying jobs, living in a small rental house, and trying to find more lucrative employment. Not a happy time.

Now we had an extra dog, which meant more dog food and vet bills.

We named the little pistol Piglet, because that's what she looked like. Piglet was stubborn, ornery and sweet all at the same time. We had no idea what to do with her, but we weren't about to take her to the pound or a shelter. The fine folks there had their hands full.

Piglet lived with us for a month or so, until we went to a flea market and offered her to "a good home."

A somewhat careworn young woman with dirty babies asked to take Piglet for her own pet. We handed Piglet over and wished them all the best.

Mission accomplished.

Or was it?

We will never know whether Piglet lived out a healthy and happy life, because we simply didn't know what we were doing. To this day I wonder.

Piglet was the first of a long string of stray pets my husband and I, and later our children, have picked up and recycled to new homes. Four hundred dogs, cats and the occasional bird later, we've gotten better at this, more confident, more at ease, more ready, and more strict. And, yes, it has gotten easier. Now I'm prepared to impart our experience to you, so you can easily and confidently help stray animals in your area, without getting stuck with big bills or an extra pet you don't want, or can't afford.

Foster parents, of kids or pets, are heroes. There's strain, expense, and heartbreak involved with fostering, though balanced quite effectively by peace of mind, personal satisfaction, a boost for the ego, and just plain old-fashioned good works. Helping a stray, whether human or animal, gives the giver a heightened sense of worth. In fact, you end up with much better control over your life and your world than you may imagine. You become a doer, not a spectator in life.

All this from a little mutt eating sidewalk cigarette butts thirty-odd years ago? Darn right.

Know thyself

Don't keep stray pets! You don't have to. If you like animals, you probably have pets already. You do not have to keep additional pets just because you want to help strays. Prepare yourself by setting an absolute limit on how many animals you will have as permanent pets and how many others you will

Children adjust to stray pets' coming and going, and themselves become part of the solution. They are especially good at exercising and socializing strays. Children understand having a mission.

help at any one time. We have restricted ourselves to owning one dog and one cat, leaving room to help temporary animal guests without being overwhelmed. We have stuck to that. Our personal pets deserve to have their homes and us to themselves, and to live without chaos. It's best for the guests, too. Having pets is definitely not a "the more, the merrier" situation.

Sometimes this best-laid plan is fouled by a pet with puppies or kittens, but you can prepare for that or learn to deal with it when it happens.

Decide to do it

The first and biggest step in helping stray animals is actually making the decision to help them. The simple mantra, "Next time, I will try," will prepare you to act the next time you spot an animal in need. This requires mentally dispensing with the typical excuses: "I'm in a hurry," "It's probably somebody's pet," "Somebody else will help" and "He'll find his way home."

Before you can pick up a stray animal, you should be prepared mentally and physically, because spotting a stray happens in an instant. If you're not mentally geared to take action, you'll be a mile past the problem before you realize you could have done something.

You're rushing along in your car, on your way to somewhere. You're a little late, but not quite ready to increase speed. Suddenly a motion in your periphery catches your attention. A flash of color against the shoulder of the road—it's a dog! Right out in the open next to speeding traffic, he's sniffing, moving erratically, going in one direction for a few steps, then back in another direction, even dodging cars.

"Awww… " you moan.

You'd like to help. You really would. But—

EXCUSE: I'm in a hurry!

Of course you're in a hurry. We're all in a hurry. If you weren't going somewhere, you wouldn't be in your car.

Later, you're haunted by the image of the confused, desperate, endangered dog or cat, obviously in trouble, with no *human* hand to steady his troubles. How can you banish these awful thoughts, which sometimes last years?

Ask yourself: Can I be a little late? Won't those waiting for me understand? You know perfectly well that most of the time, you do have the time to be a good samaritan. That's why you feel guilty telling yourself "I'm in a hurry" or making up other excuses. You know the real reason you don't stop is that you just don't want to make what may be an inconvenient and even expensive commitment.

Admit sooner than later that you do have ten minutes to spare for a helpless animal. And when you see that creature in need, spend those ten minutes you put in the bank. Unless you're on the way to the hospital to have a baby, you have the time--and you know it.

Get used to the idea of pulling over and making that ol' college try—visualize the action before the situation arises the next time. See yourself pressing the brake and steering the car to the side of the road, so you'll be ready when the time comes.

EXCUSE: It's probably somebody's pet.

Yes! Of course it's somebody's pet! Or was. All domesticated animals belong to somebody!

But where is that somebody? He's not watching his pet, that's for sure. So, maybe its lost or abandoned. Either way, if the pet is not being watched, then he needs human help. Yours.

Resolve this: "I will not be surprised the next time I see a stray dog. I'll know what to do. I'll put my foot on the brake and pull to the side of the road. Then I can assess the situation calmly, rather than instantly at forty-five miles an hour." Be ready to pull over.

EXCUSE: Somebody else will help.

Maybe. That's what I said to myself when I passed a large white dog on an expressway near my home years ago. I was on my way to a job interview and talked myself out of stopping. I was in my best clothes, high heels, and it was summer outside the air conditioning of my car. Wind blowing, sweltering heat, smelly traffic... Stop to help a dog?

Somebody else would help.

I arrived at the job interview ten minutes early and sat there thinking about the dog. The interview wouldn't start for another fifteen minutes. More time to think.

On the way home, I saw the dog again. He had been hit by a car and killed.

It's twenty years later. I didn't get the job. I don't even remember what kind of job the interview was about. However, I've never forgotten the white dog. I wish I'd stopped.

Don't expect somebody else to help. You're "it."

Be somebody.

EXCUSE: He'll find his way home.

If the pet could find his way home, he would already *be* home. There are anecdotes and even movies about pets separated from their owners, only to miraculously turn up weeks or months later. This happens, but not often. In today's urbanized environment of concrete, speeding cars, metal fences, waterways and endless miles of highway, the likelihood that a lost pet will stumble back on something he recognizes is virtually zero. Real *Incredible Journeys* are dismally rare. Being lost in the human world is brutal for a stray animal.

Don't tell yourself childhood fibs to make yourself feel better. Dogs and cats are not wolves or lions. They are completely domesticated pets, as helpless in the wild or anywhere else as dairy cows and barn chickens. They were bred to live comfortably with us. They've lost their ability to live feral lives and remain healthy.

Even feral dogs and cats around the world are frequently ill, hungry and short-lived. They don't grow the kinds of winter coats we imagine they do, nor can they endure long periods of summer heat without clean water and cool shelter.

That's humanity's doing, and therefore it's humanity's responsibility to help these dependent creatures we bred to need us. Decide to do it! Take charge.

Deciding to help a stray animal has to happen *before* you see the next one. You have to be ready in your mind, or the pet's confusion, fear and desperation becomes yours too. Head off that confusion by making a decision to take action and seize the situation. Be decisive. Say it out loud to yourself. Hearing the words actually does help:

"Next time I see a pet that seems to be without supervision, I will take charge. The decision is made. I'm ready."

CHECKLIST

❑ Decide that you will stop the next time you see a stray dog or cat.

❑ Prepare by imagining what you will do when you see that animal.

❑ Ignore the excuses, and act.

Old Santa Dundee was adopted by the Carey-Brodeur family at six months old, and lived to be fifteen years old. Not bad for a dog who was one day from euthanasia at the pound.

Lesson 2

COMPASSION IS NOT A CHARACTER FLAW

Wanting to help stray pets doesn't make you a weak person, an "animal nut" or a bleeding-heart sucker. A person who wants to pick up stray pets certainly isn't looking for accolades or to shirk responsibility off onto others, or a handout.

Those of us who feel desperate, worried or confused when we see a roaming dog or cat are not "animal nuts." Animal nuts have no self-control and find themselves with twenty cats in each bedroom. Compassion isn't a sign of a weak or whimsical nature. In my experience, after more than four hundred strays, this little "hobby" has shown itself to take a special hardening of personal sensitivity and a backpack full of courage, strictness and self-restraint. There are tough decisions to be made, expenses to deal with and new skills to learn. You must develop the guts to do it.

But when you do... you feel better about yourself to a degree that is difficult to quantify. Helping the helpless is therapeutic and empowering. You may find yourself feeling more in control of other situations in your life.

Taking extra steps in life pushes us out of our personal

envelopes and stretches our wings. Something as menial as helping stray pets makes you aware of details, helps you handle money more efficiently, presses you to make contacts with people you otherwise would never meet, and gains you respect from others.

The effect ripples.

I became reacquainted with a good friend from my old neighborhood, only to discover that she had taken my example years ago. She shops around pounds and shelters for dogs of certain breeds, buys their freedom, tends their sicknesses, sees to their training, and bravely seeks out excellent new homes for them. This process sometimes takes as much as a year. I'm proud of her and her family, and proud of myself for providing an example—even if it was unintended.

Humans—Americans in particular—too often beat ourselves up as heartless, greedy and destructive. We're poisoning the land, killing the oceans, wrecking the reefs, drying the wet lands, ignoring the helpless, starving the children—name the transgression and we will see it in ourselves. Humans are scum, animals are pristine.

Now for a reality check

Animals do not clean up after themselves. Humans do. Humans are the only creatures who purposefully recycle, struggle to beat back the extinction of other species than our own, work to correct damage by ourselves and nature itself, and keep an eye on each other's errors or crimes and battle to diminish them.

Humans are the only animals who look out for other animals, sometimes with great expense, effort and sacrifice. Many creatures would no longer exist but for the aggression of humanity and preservations efforts enacted by humans. This happens not in spite of our much-denounced modern industrial society, but *because* of it. The sheer dynamism of entrepreneurial spirit has created enormous companies that devote millions, even billions, annually to clean-ups, preservation, mitigation and conservation. It has also created a society of people who are well enough off financially to be able to help other people and other animals. Poverty is not noble; it's just poverty. Wealth is not evil; in fact, it's the root of all good.

Only a successful society can afford to help creatures other than themselves.

We've had a depressed economy for several years, in America and likewise around the world. Greg and I lived in Flint, Michigan, a city plagued with poor leadership, crushing debt, and widespread dependence on government handouts. We noticed that as the economy failed, the first thing to be thrown out was the family pet. The higher the unemployment rate and welfare dependence, the more pets my husband and I picked up or acquired from neighbors who were not caring for them. It was very hard for us, of course, because we were picking up someone else's burdens while we had our own to carry. We bore the weight of other people's irresponsibility and their quick way out: dump the dog or cat. We could gauge the state of the economy around us by how many dogs and cats we were seeing on the streets. The link was obvious and tragic. As more and more people abandoned their responsibility to take care of themselves and their own children, more and more pets suffered.

Unlike many other places, America offers its poor one great gift: the chance to get rich if you work for it. This dynamic society gives us the chance, the time, and the money to throw some of our good fortune toward bettering the condition of stray animals on the street. We have the right to pursue happiness, but not at the expense of others, and not by shoving our responsibilities off on our neighbors. We must get up off our duffs and *pursue*.

Too many people have been taught the wrong message: that someone else should pay, should shoulder the weight of their neighbors' bad choices, and that includes unwanted pets and the offspring of unspayed pets. The more people riding the wagon, the harder it is to tow for the rest of us.

Next time you feel the twinge of empathy for some living creature who needs help, be glad you are American and free to take action. Square your shoulders and feel good that you are part of the human race, the only animal that bothers to help other animals.

That twinge is a call to action.

CHECKLIST

❏ Don't take any crap from others about being an "animal nut." Just respond, "We must be humane to be good humans."

❏ If you don't have a job, get one. Any job. There is no such thing as "a dead-end job." All jobs are productive, no matter how menial. If you help yourself by working, you will help your children's sense of self-esteem and respect for you, and you will have the means to help stray pets when you see them.

Keisha and one of her puppies, Buffy. I accepted Keisha when her pups were only one day old, raised them to eight weeks, and found new families for them.

Lesson 3

BE PREPARED TO DO IT

Physically, you should have items in your car and home that will assist you. Preparing your house as well as your car makes for minimal disruption of your home life and your own pets' lives.

The best way to do that is to be prepared. Go out and buy a

cheap leash, collars, some dog food or treats, and some cat food in cans with a pull-open lid. Get an old blanket to protect your car's back seat. Get some old tennis shoes in case you have to do a little walking to capture a stray. Get some thick work gloves so you're not hurt if the animal bites or scratches. Carry a raincoat, hat, and slip-on boots in the trunk in case you have to go out in bad weather. If you take care of yourself, you'll be in a much better condition to help a stray.

One item is valuable: a good knife. Purchase or acquire a strong, sharp utility knife or razor knife and keep it in the center console next to the driver's seat. If you're in an accident or happen upon an accident that has just happened, you may want to cut a seat belt to free yourself or someone else. If you find a stray pet in a trapped situation, caught in wire or fencing, you'll have a way to free it. A good Swiss Army knife or other type of rescue knife is an excellent emergency tool.

At home, if you have a fenced in yard, great. If not, you may want to purchase a screw-in hook for a long leash, and a long leash to go with it, so you can put a stray dog outside comfortably and safely.

Most of these items, and much more, can be found at any dollar store.

Write your name on a small piece of paper and securely tape it to the pet's collar. You are this animal's second chance; if he gets away from you, his chances get worse and you'll feel bad. If he has a phone number on him, he will be back in a very short time. Doing this is part of preparing your mind; you have taken charge of this unfortunate creature. You are now responsible for his future. It's a burden, yes, but also a gift for your self-confidence and your sense of command in a world of chaos. You'll get used to it.

No one expects you to become the patron saint of pets overnight, but there are small steps to take which turn from someone who drives on by and feels terrible later into someone who takes charge, who imparts control to an uncontrolled situation, and who feels great later.

You'll be different at the end of this book. You'll be happier!

CHECKLIST

❑ Help the next time you see a stray pet.

❑ Prepare your car.

❑ Prepare your mind.

❑ Prepare your house.

In your car, keep a good knife, cheap leash, two or three collars of different sizes, treats, a pull-open can of food, work gloves and an old blanket. A raincoat, boots, old shoes and a fishing net to catch cats are also recommended.

In your house, keep a pet bed, screw-in lease hook for the yard, a long line with a clip at the end, pet food and a baby gate to keep the pet restricted to one room inside the house.

Our first permanent dog, beautiful flat-coated retriever Sharvan, "the
Ava Gardner" of the neighborhood, as our neighbors dubbed her.

Lesson 4

SHARVAN

My mother's neighbor in 1978 was a dogand-cat lover and had enough money to do something about it. During January of 1979, my now-husband Greg Brodeur and I were newly engaged and living in that little rental house, pooling our nominal resources and building toward an October wedding. Our lives were not exactly settled, but we now had a real house instead of an apartment. Piglet wasn't our first stray, strictly speaking. While living in an Ann Arbor, Michigan apartment during my master's studies, I picked up two dogs, a hound and a cocker roaming on the expressway. We found the hound's owner, but the cocker, a perfectly adorable dog, had to be given to a new home. I started with Piglet, because she was our first real commitment, the first dog we actually decided to help, and were determined to help.

Just before we found Piglet, I had informed my reluctant fiancé that I was taking a big black dog that the mother's neighbor, whose name was also Diane, had found running stray in a friend's neighborhood. Diane had seen this young dog playing with children and generally hanging around. As winter approached, she had decided to take charge. She had taken the dog home, had medical treatment and shots administered, absorbed the vet bills, and now had a healthy extra dog on her hands which she did not want to keep.

The young black dog was utterly gorgeous. She was pure coal-black and with silky long hair, built exactly like an Irish setter. For years we thought she was actually a black Irish setter, because there are white, black, and red-and-white Irish setters. She was not a Gordon either, a heavier-boned breed that I have now. We discovered years later that she was in fact a flat-coated retriever, a little-known breed which finally took best-of-breed in a major dog show and has become somewhat better known and accepted by the American Kennel Club.

Flat-coated retrievers are wonderful family dogs, excellent with children, cheerful and loving, though as a bird-hunting breed, they do need quite a bit of exercise.

As a puppy, this particular dog had been owned by someone in the neighborhood where she was found, but she had a habit of running off. The owners didn't bother to stop the running problem. Finally, when the dog went missing for a few days, they got another dog, this time a black setter pup came home. It didn't take long before the pup was no longer welcome.

Unfed and unattended, she haunted the neighborhood loyally for the last three of her nine months, growing up on the street somehow, expecting her "parents" to change their minds. She must have been fed now and then by someone, or she wouldn't have survived. But she was a stray.

Now she was ours. Her giant black eyes and beautiful silky ears flinched in some confusion as we drove her home in our '66 Ventura. Her head was perfectly shaped, like a sculptor's model of a beautiful bird dog. She had a long nose, flowing black ears, huge black chestnut eyes, and the posture of a queen.

We called her Sharvan, a name I made up that sounded

Irish. She had a face like Cleopatra, the elegant demeanor of Ava Gardner, the heart of a teddy bear and the brain of a block of wood. Well, might as well be honest. Setters aren't the brightest bulbs in the box. I mean, really, we're not talking about a border collie or a poodle here. They have huge hearts of gold, but they're dopes.

Big-hearted Sharvan loved and trusted us to an amazing degree. She was cuddly despite her size, affectionate as a baby. Despite her size, she was still a puppy. A one-year-old dog is not an adult yet. Flat-coated retrievers and setters have the amiable quality of remaining puppies in their minds and behavior all their lives.

Sharvan loved children. The only time she defied us was to get to a child. We assumed children had been kind to her during her wild period, and she simply adored them.

Our house butted up against a large untended meadow. Every evening, Greg would come home to Sharvan's delicate black feet pounding the carpet in excitement.

"Go to the field, Sharvan?" he would say, "Go to the field?"

Sharvan's long drawl out *wooo-wooooooo* of happiness gave us our daily dose of laughter during a stressful time. (The only thing more hilarious than a big dog's trying to understand English is a big dog's trying to *speak* English.)

She ran like a whip of smoke in the wind. She crashed in and out of the tall weeds and meadow grasses with merry abandon, flushing pheasants and sparrows in a spectacular scene like something out of an English hunt painting. "Going to the field" became a nightly ritual.

One day she was busily flushing some pheasants and broke out of the meadowgrass with a squawking bird right in her mouth. She pranced happily toward us, not quite understanding that there was a pheasant in her mouth. The bird was righteously indignant about the whole incident.

After a few seconds, Sharvan got the idea that the bird's cussing was aimed at her. She dropped the pheasant and pranced in a circle, pleased with her prowess and pretty surprised that she'd actually caught one. The bird flew off, voicing quite another opinion.

This was one wonderful dog.

She was also completely untrained. Our beautiful Sharvan was a full year old and *not housebroken*.

Puppies make moist little piddles and annoying little piles. Year-old setters make great big puddles and enormous smelly piles. No fun.

Even then, I wouldn't have a dog tied up outside all day or all night. Dogs belong inside with their pack. The weather was too cold to tie her in the yard even during the day while we worked or looked for jobs out of town, so Sharvan spent the days inside. Since we too were young and didn't have the brains to ask a neighbor to let her out a couple of times a day (such a simple solution!) we pretty much came home every night to a mess.

She had been a wild dog for six months and she was still young and teething. She destroyed every pair of shoes I owned, one at a time. We had no idea what to do.

Getting rid of Sharvan was out of the question. First, we had made a commitment to her. That's what happens when you adopt a child or a dog. Usually it's the adoptive parents who need training just as much as an adoptee. Most pets end up in shelters or pounds because the *people* are not properly trained to have a pet or deal with pet problems. If I had Sharvan now, I would know exactly what to do. But back then, we didn't even have the brains to ask for help.

Second, she needed us. Animals are helpless in today's modern world. A stray pet has already used up its first chance and is hoping for a second. To take Sharvan to a shelter or pound would have been a death warrant. Shelters have a hard time finding homes for all dogs, especially large dogs—and especially

Be proud of yourself for being part of the solution.

black dogs.

Third, we loved her. She loved us.

We sacrificed the shoes and dealt with the mess. We later realized that part of the piddle/poop problem was the carpet in the rental house. The previous tenants had had cats, and the cats had soiled in the carpet. With only her canine olfactory talents to depend upon, Sharvan couldn't tell inside from outside. She had no idea why she was being disciplined for piddling inside. Inside and outside smelled alike to her. What she did made perfect sense to her, and she didn't understand why she was being swatted and scolded. Her owners weren't trained.

Instead, we cleaned up mess after mess and destruction after destruction. Six months later, we moved into a house with wood floors. Lo—no more inside piddles or piles! Sharvan quickly came to understand that in and out were different. Such a simple solution—if only we'd known.

Sharvan had another problem... she tended to run off. Of course she did; she had run wild for the entire second half of her life. Running free was normal for her. The idea of a yard with boundaries was simply alien. Our new house had no fence, though we soon built one around the back yard. However, once out in the front yard, Sharvan would still take off for parts unknown. We were trying to teach her about our yard and staying near us, so we would let her roam the front yard and try to keep an eye on her, calling her back when she overstepped. Despite our efforts, once in a while she would slip away.

A dog who is constantly confined in fences or tied up never learns that from-here-to-there is his yard boundary. Only once allowed to be in the yard without restraint will a dog learn its immediate territory. Some learn faster than others. Sharvan knew our house and our yard. She would never leave while we were with her. We could freely take walks or go to parks without a leash. She always stayed with us.

But... we lived between two schools. Remember—Sharvan adored children. Oops.

When Sharvan went out into the front yard in the morning, she would occasionally disappear. We soon learned we could go straight to the school grounds and she would be in one of them. Every school child for blocks around knew Sharvan. She would pick them up in our yard and walk them to their schools. Then, of course, the bell would ring and the children would go inside, leaving Sharvan alone on the grounds.

We consistently worked on the idea of boundaries. When Sharvan ventured into neighbors' yards, we would call her back. Consistency in our manner and effort was the ticket. It took that one element so many pet owners are unwilling to give: *time,*

and lots of it. One day, like the soft stroke of a magic wand—
bing—she got the idea. I could almost see a light go off in her
not-particularly-large brain. "Oh! The yard goes from here to
here! I get it!"

From then on, Sharvan would escort the children from
one end of the yard to the other, pick up another group, and
walk them back. Once she got the idea, she had it for good. She
never ran away again. Her only big transgression was lying in
the street with her long legs stretched out, raising her head like
royalty and woofing at cars.

"Sharvan, go to the field!" remained our daily chant. Because
of Sharvan, Greg and I got in a very good habit—a long walk
every night, rain or shine, winter or summer. Our dog had
prompted us into what would be a lifetime of good exercise and
a daily chance to unwind and just talk to each other, which we
still enjoy to this day.

We had no meadow, but lived between two parks. At
these parks, Sharvan discovered a miracle: squirrels don't fly.
Bounding with delight, she chased squirrel after squirrel in
the parks as she grew from a big puppy into an elegant and
somewhat more coordinated setter.

Then, one day, instinct kicked in. Sharvan saw a squirrel,
but instead of just running full out and announcing her presence
with a rush, she suddenly went on point. Her head went down,
her sleek nose went out, her back made a straight line and her
beautiful triangular tail went straight out behind her. Her long
legs froze in place, and her front leg came up. She was the perfect
picture of a hunter.

Cars would slow to a halt in the middle of the road. Parents
and children would stop playing. Pedestrians would pause to
watch. Sharvan was worth watching as she ever so slowly and
patiently stepped toward whatever hapless squirrel she had spied.

Finally she would break into a charge. The squirrel would
come to life and dart up a tree. Sharvan would just barely miss

the squirrel, then circle the tree, barking in delighted frustration. The people around us would laugh and applaud. Sharvan made a great show. Occasionally she would actually catch and kill a squirrel, but this was *very* rare. Mostly the point, stalk and charge was the big excitement of "the field."

Once trained to stay in our yard and not to wizz in the house, Sharvan the stray, Sharvan the untrained, Sharvan the big dog who would be too much trouble for a house transformed into the world's most perfect pet. She was quiet, she was peaceful, she was beautiful, she loved us in a way that demonstrated itself with every glancea nd she taught us that anyone who believes dogs are just bio-machines running on instinct alone are full of manure. This was not a captive boa constrictor. This was a member of our family.

Sharvan, once a stray roaming free, undisciplined and untrained, lived eleven years until she sadly contracted melanoma cancer, a common disease for flat-coated retrievers. To this day she remains our most-adored and sorely missed pet, almost a child. She welcomed two babies into our home and was gentle with both, and with all children. Even two dogs and many strays later, we still miss her and are glad she came into our lives.

Checklist

❏ Learn to train the particular breed of pet you have chosen.

❏ Seek advice from groups that rescue that breed.

❏ Adopt a black dog.

Lesson 5

PREPARE THYSELF (AND THY FAMILY)

D on't just rush out and start picking up dogs and cats.

Mention to your family that you've decided to take charge if this situation arises. Mention that you'd like to take a shot at helping rather than just driving by next time. Tell your spouse you intend to pull over, whether you're driving or not. Nothing may come of it, but you're going to pull over and assess the situation. Can't hurt to stop the car for a few minutes. That way, there are no surprises or arguments. Everyone has time to adjust to the idea.

State flat-out that you don't intend to keep any pets you pick up. Believe it yourself. Your lifestyle and theirs won't radically change. You won't be overrun with mutts. You're just going to try to be a halfway house for critters who could really use the help.

Reactions will differ. Some family members may leap to the chance of helping the helpless. Others will instantly resist. "What? Bring dirty, smelly, unmedicated, stray animals into *this* house? Forget it!"

Okay, so you may have to adjust the lifestyle of the garage instead of the house. You can still do this.

You'll make a few preparations and adjustments to be ready when you find a stray pet. These won't be obvious or expensive, but will make your job far easier when the time comes. Here's the list:

The Guest Room

Prepare a kind of "guest room" for your future waifs. If you think you may pick up cats, prepare a restricted indoor area with soft beds, a litter box, litter, some dry cat food, and a scratching post. These things are available very cheaply at garage sales or dollar stores. Tuck them away.

If you think you'll welcome dogs, get a dog house or make an area in the garage, shed or basement where a stray dog can get out of the weather. The area should be shaded, warm in winter, cool in summer, and wind-protected. There must be some kind of dry thick pad, bean bag, heavy blanket or cushion for the pet to use as a bed. No dog or cat is well off sleeping on bare ground or concrete. Their joints and bones need cushioning as much as yours do.

Pets should not sleep outside! Even in summer, there are the problems of dew, humidity, excessive heat, moisture, harassment by kids or other animals, uncontrolled barking and just plain loneliness. Domesticated dogs and cats are meant to be with people.

Winter is out of the question. Even outside doghouses, sheds or garages are not enough protection from a North American winter. Remember, dogs and cats are not wolves or lions. They do not grow the kinds of coats necessary for temperature extremes. Their legs, paws, eyes, noses and undersides are not tempered for it. They have been domesticated to need protection from the weather as much as we do, and they should sleep inside.

Have a small stock of chew bones, treats, and rawhide chewies on hand, so your new friend doesn't chew your possessions.

Get a few tags and collars. Your stray should always be tagged or at least have your phone number on. At many stores and hardwares, you can get inexpensive engraved pet tags. Have two or three made that just say, *I'm lost. Please call [your number]*.

Put them right on the collars you're going to keep in your car trunk. Or just tape a small piece of paper with information onto a couple of collars and have them ready. As long as your stray has a phone number, he will never be alone again.

CHECKLIST

❑ Discuss your plans with your family.

❑ Get a litter box ready.

❑ Buy cat food.

❑ Get a scratching post.

❑ Get chew bones or rawhides.

❑ Create a solid, weatherproof shelter in your house or garage.

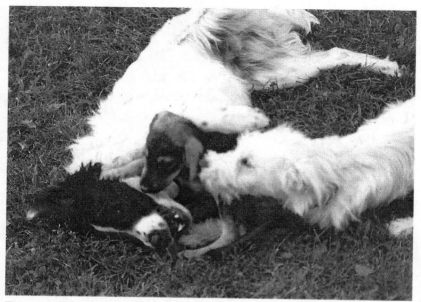

These three young dogs were rescued at the same time and became a "litter" together, helping to replace the litter mates they had lost. This is very good for young pets' adjustment.

Lesson 6

YOU ARE NOT ALONE

We all feel alone and secluded when a helpless animal falls into our paws. It helps to know there are others like us.

Make friends with your local humane organization and even with your local animal control officers. They'll be a good source of other people like you, folks who pick up and help strays. A network of folks like us can be a great boon when one of us needs help. After all, you may see a stray just after you break an ankle and can't take care of a waif. It helps to be able to call someone who will probably take your guest off your hands.

You may offer a couple hours a week as a volunteer at your local animal shelter. You'll gain contacts and earn trust in the community. You'll also become more at ease with handling unfamiliar animals and their problems. You'll become more experienced and confident. If you're a participating member of the animal rescue network—and an hour or two here and there will do it—you're more likely to feel powerful rather than desperate when a stray dog or cat comes your way.

You may also stage helpful events such as garage sales or bake sales to the benefit of your local shelter. Have your friends donate items to sell, and put up a big sign: PROCEEDS TO ANIMAL SHELTER.

Offer to let the shelter bring some pets to show.

If these are too much for you, ask if you can assist at an event they already have planned. Once you've helped them, they're very likely to help you.

CHECKLIST

❑ Locate an animal rescue and foster group in your area.

❑ Get to know people by participating in fundraising.

❑ Build a support network so you don't feel alone.

Our first rescued cat, Simmony, lived to be 18 years old and raised our kids to love cats.

Lesson 7

WHITE-FACED SIMMONY

A pair of newlyweds out for donuts in January. No big deal, right? Nothing earth-shattering.

I had never owned a cat. My childhood neighborhood had no cats. Nobody even had an indoor cat, never mind cats running the neighborhood. I know there were no cats far and wide, because we had two enormous sandboxes which would've been compromised.

The only cat I recall belonged to my Auntie Elishua, not really my aunt but my grandmother's best friend. This lovely round old Assyrian lady was one of the sweetest people I've ever known, and she had a friendly smoke-gray cat named Puffer with a gigantic fluffy tail.

Puffer provided my only exposure to cats, which seemed like a pretty strange life form to me. I was a dog person. I knew dogs. I understood dogs. I had raised dogs. I sketched dogs. I dreamed of having big elegant dogs with flowing hair and kingly stature.

When Greg and I got together, his parents lived in West Bloomfield, Michigan and seemed to have a cat, a Siamese named Spider. I say "seemed to," because Spider had actually adopted the Brodeur family instead of the other way around. Spider had belonged to someone else in the fairly exclusive subdivision, but continually sought out the Brodeur kids—all seven of them—because of the playful harassment he received from them. Yes, the concept of a Siamese cat as aloof and solitary is soundly thrashed by memory of Spider. This is a cat that would run around in the backyard playing badminton with the sizable herd of Brodeurs.

Spider decided he wanted to live with the Brodeurs and that's where he hung out. For some mystical reason, Greg's mom bought kitty litter for him, despite the fact that Spider was outside whenever he wanted to be. I witnessed this wildcat rushing across the beautiful green lawns of the interconnected backyards, dashing into the sliding doorway someone opened for him, and racing to his litter box. Amazing. With all of Mother Nature to use as a toilet, this self-motivated cat had somehow conned a family into providing him a porta-potty in their laundry room.

Well, this was a cat. I had no cat experience. Thus my amazement when Greg played "Spin the Cat."

Spider would haunt Greg until he flattened the cat out on his side on the linoleum hallway floor and rigorously began spinning him. Spider's legs would fan out, his eyes glaze over in pleasure, and away they went. This was a Siamese? One of the most sophisticated breeds around?

Spider's owners finally came over to the Brodeurs and said, "Fine. He's your cat. Good luck."

While packing to move to Florida, Greg's mother was carrying a cardboard box containing something she found interesting enough to show to each person in the family room, one by one. She almost got out of the room, when Spider, who was lying like the Pharaoh against a wall, let out a strict "*Mrrrrow!*"

Without a pause Greg's mom said, "Oh, all right!" She bent down with the box.

Spider stretched upward and looked into the box. Then—and only then—was Mom allowed to leave the room. After all, everybody else had looked in.

I wouldn't have believed it if I hadn't seen it for myself. Was this the way all cats were? Smart? In control? This was definitely not behavior a dog person understood. Dogs are happy if you just throw them a kind word and a piece of bacon. This cat, though, was determined to be taken as an equal member of the Brodeur family.

Spider moved to Florida with Greg's parents and the two youngest Brodeurs. He lived to a ripe old age, ruling the Cocoa Beach condo as efficiently as he had ruled the big house in West Bloomfield.

In time, Greg and I married and settled into our pleasant corner house on Cadillac Street in Flint, Michigan, with our big black Sharvan. The two of us and the dog of my dreams. Perfect. No adjustments necessary.

Until January. Outside the Dawn Donuts shop on Pierson Road in my old haunts in west Flint, we discovered a movement against the new snow—a pure white cat, about six months old. This cat was friendly, bright-eyed, looking around with a healthy nervous curiosity. I knelt to greet the cat and found myself peering into an odd set of eyes, one sky blue, and one lemon yellow.

There was no one else around. The cat scanned traffic continuously, but was relieved to rest in my arms. After a few moments, he made a little broken meow that sounded more like "Ah—ow?" He never quite got the "mee" part. I figured he must be pleasantly unselfish.

"He's lost," I declared.

My much wiser husband said, "Diane, cats roam for miles.

He's not necessarily lost."

All my instincts, though, said this cat didn't know where he was. I would take him home. I did, without having any idea how Sharvan and this cat would tolerate each other. We walked in the door, Sharvan's beautiful black head popped up, and the cat's eyes got big. The dog wanted out, the cat wanted in, and that was all it took. They accepted each other.

I didn't bother naming the white kitty, because he wouldn't be here long. We would recirculate him to a new home. I wrote an ad and placed it in the local paper.

In the meantime, this white cat with the two-colored eyes settled into our home as if he'd always been here. After a day, we went back to the Dawn Donuts, just in case anybody happened to be searching for the white cat with the blue eye and the yellow eye. The lady behind the counter said, "Nobody wants him. I saw him get pushed out of a car window. He waited all day for his owners to come back. We gave him some milk."

The cruel bottom-feeders who tossed the white cat out their car window will never know what a truly wonderful pet he turned out to be. The tragedy is that he almost never got the chance.

Greg tells a story, first to me and then to our children, which came to him as a child. It is the tale of the mansion High Top A-Mountain, a place where water and fire have funny names like Cocolorum and Pundalorum, where food is Squibs and Crackers, and where the cat is called White-Faced Simmony. I found myself nightly gazing into a white face with a blue eye and a yellow eye as this calm little man rested on my chest while I lay on the couch to watch TV. Was this White-Faced Simmony? No, because we weren't keeping the cat. We didn't want a cat. We weren't ready for a cat. We'd never had a cat... Keep talking, right?

Along comes Friday. The ad comes out. I'm watching TV on the couch. The white cat is on my chest. The phone rings.

Greg answers. Yes, it's somebody who's interested in this

white male six-month-old cat.

I never took the phone. I looked up at Greg, put out a lip, and said, "But I want him."

Greg muffles the phone and dons his best pay-attention-or-else expression. "Di... cats live *twenty years*."

"I want him."

Greg puts the phone to his ear. "Sorry, the cat has a home."

White-Faced Simmony had found his High Top A-Mountain. Within two weeks he had made his visit to the vet to be neutered, which he took in surprising stride. Simmony took everything in stride.

Sporting his new blue collar and ID tag, Simmony soon discovered the kitty litter box moving closer to the back door, then finally right out the door. After a while, it disappeared, but by then he was perfectly accustomed to doing his business outside. He soon made friends in the neighborhood, from the two elderly ladies on Perry Street who fed him hot dinner every night to the squirrels he chased across our garage roof. Those ladies would become good friends to us, helping and advising when we picked up strays over the next few years. They were Mrs. Bennett and Mrs. Bennett, Lolita and Leona, blood sisters who had married blood brothers. Now widowed, they lived three houses down. It wasn't unusual for one of them to call and say, "Send Sharvan down. Her dinner's ready."

The Bennetts also picked up strays, or just other people's free-roaming cats. There were many cats who called the Bennett garage home. Simmony would frequently hang out there. Being in their eighties, the ladies could pretty much do as they pleased without fear of getting in trouble. They were known to pick up cats living in our neighborhood, take those cats to the vet, have them spayed or neutered, then simply turn them loose again. Irresponsible owners would find their cats missing for a few days, only to reappear later. Those people probably had no idea why their cats never contributed to unwanted kittens. The

Bennetts had pluck.

Husband Greg sensed right away what kind of woman he had married. I would have fifteen cats and twenty dogs if he didn't put a strap on this soft-hearted gene I was born with. He struck a deal with me: I could pick up strays, as long as I kept our household down to one permanent dog and one permanent cat.

Simmony and Sharvan became good friends, frequently even sleeping in the same bed.

Of course, we took Sharvan "to the field" every night—a good long walk around our sprawling neighborhood to Mott Park and back. One evening, before we picked up our pace toward Chevrolet Avenue, I stopped to tie my shoe. The movement caused me to turn around.

Peering at me from the gray night sidewalk was a small white face. A little broken meow greeted me through the evening air. Simmony, in a very uncatlike manner, was trailing us. How long had he been following on our walks? We had no idea.

A pretty rosy-cheeked baby named Lydia Rose was born on a hot June day in 1983. Sharvan wanted to kiss her, and the baby loved lying up against Sharvan's velvety black side. For being all legs and heart—still no brain registering on the meter—Sharvan was delicately attentive around the baby, even when the baby's fingers poked into her eyes.

Lydia and Simmony were best friends. When Lydia was four years old, this sensible little moppet with an eye toward fantasy and a mind for numbers decided her father and I had committed some injustice or other and she would move out. She began packing all her stuffed toys into her My Little Pony suitcase. "I'm going to live with Mandy."

The best friend lived on the other corner of our block. There would be justice at Mandy's.

Greg asked what Lydia thought he and Mommy would do without her. No effect.

"What's Simmony going to do without you?" he asked.

Lydia dissolved into tears.

"Don't talk about Simmony!" she sobbed, and drifted into her daddy's arms.

Thus, the white fuzzball we'd found outside the Dawn Donuts became our hero when he prevented our pre-school daughter from joining the Foreign Legion. Well done, White-Faced Simmony.

Checklist

❑ Learn to love cats.

❑ Learn to love dogs.

❑ But learn to love them enough to keep only a couple for yourself.

Dogs and cats are domesticated pets, not wild animals. They are
critically endangered when running "free," and need to be taken off
the streets for their own good, and the general health of society.

Lesson 8

PLAY IT SAFE

O n the road, in parking lots, or in the backyard, you may stumble upon a lost pet almost anywhere. I've found strays rushing up to my car trailing a leash, or hiding under sports bleachers. Generally speaking, the two most likely places you'll see a wandering pet is while you're in your car or in your house. As noted in previous chapters, both your car and your house should be ready.

How do you catch a roaming cat or dog?

Keep Yourself Safe

First, guard your own safety. Avoid crossing busy roads, climbing into unknown terrain, entering buildings, or wandering unsafe areas. If there's too big a risk involved, simply call Animal Control and let them handle it. No dog or cat is worth your life or limb.

Do not risk your life or your wellbeing for a stray animal.

That said, do try to help if the situation can be managed

safely. If the animal is on your side of the road or you can get closer to him, do so while still in the car.

Then get out and get the animal's attention. If he runs from you, there's nothing you can do. I gave up chasing dogs and cats long ago. You can't possibly catch a four-legged animal that doesn't want to be caught, unless he's hurt.

If it is hurt or cornered, you stand a heightened chance of being bitten. Whether you attempt to help in spite of this depends upon you personally: how bold you are, how much experience you've had with dogs or cats, and many other variables which can't be anticipated in the pages of this book. Use your best judgment. If you can't reach a pet or are afraid to touch it, call Animal Control. At least the pet won't be running anymore.

If a dog or cat will come to you, it's probably friendly enough to touch. Get down on one knee so you're not threatening to the pet. Eye-level is an equalizer in the mind of a dog or cat. Looming over them as humans do is taken as an attempt at domination. The moment when you're trying to gain trust and control is not the time to appear dominant.

Do the old "let him sniff your hand" thing. Don't put your face close to a strange animal; it's much better to be bitten or scratched in the hand than the eye.

If the pet seems agreeable, pat his head, then his back. Slip the collar you brought with you onto him, and he's all yours. This works more often than not.

If a dog is antsy and skittish, take more time. Be calm until he approaches you with more confidence. He will probably take his emotional cues from you. Speak in happy, inviting tones. Don't raise your voice. Most of this comes naturally.

Cats are a little squirmier and less likely to want to be picked up, slower to approach or let you approach them. Be calm and take your time. You can't catch a cat unless it's willing to be caught. If you can pet and rub the cat, slip a collar on-because you were smart enough to have a tiny collar with you-- and use it as an anchor to keep hold of the cat.

If you think you'll be picking up cats—and you'll get an idea of the kind of strays that come to your realm—you may wish to stock your car with a portable cat-carry box. This provides convenience and safety for you and a sense of security for your waif.

You'll often find that other people will stop to help you corner and capture a stray. If one person—you—steps up to the plate, others are more likely to make a try also. Accept the help, but don't necessarily give up the responsibility. If someone else seems more able to care for a stray or more experienced, you may give up your claim. Generally, it's tough to get an animal away from me once I've made the decision to help him. Occasionally, though, someone else turns up better equipped to help than I. That someone may live in the area, may have a farm—there are various considerations. You be the judge.

Checklist

❏ Be careful when approaching a strange animal. It may appear docile and then snap.

❏ Approach with your hand, slowly. Be patient.

❏ Keep your face away from the animal's.

❏ Have a collar, with your phone number already attached, ready to slip on.

❏ Don't exhaust or endanger yourself when pursuing a stray.

❏ Call the authorities if you need help catching an animal or if it appears to be ill.

❏ If you feel endangered, give up.

Be aware of your neighbors' pets and how they're being treated.
If you think a dog or cat is being ignored, speak up or call the
authorities. Yes... butt in!

Lesson 9

DO WHAT YOU CAN

Certainly there are times and situations during which you
just can't do anything to help a stray you might see. You
may be on vacation or *really* in a hurry, or the pet may run into
an area you do not choose to enter. Or you're visiting Canada,
but you live in the U.S. and can't bring a pet over the border
when you come home. Understandable.

If you really can't stop, at least make a phone call. Phone the
local shelter or animal control agency and inform them of the
pet's location. He'll stand a chance of getting off the street.

If you can stop and can get to the pet, take him off the street and deliver him to the local humane organization or animal control. Explain that you're not responsible, but you didn't want the animal roaming and helpless. Humane organizations may require a donation to drop off a pet. Chalk it up to the price of decency. They need the money and you need the peace of mind. This is what your emergency pet-saving fund is for.

Humane organizations offer a better chance for a pet's future than public pounds, simply because they tend to hold onto a pet as long as possible. Most animal control agencies are overwhelmed and can't afford to keep pets longer than a certain, fairly strict time limit. However, many animal control officers are compassionate and will do their best within the limits of their funding.

In any case, even the pound is better than the street. The animal may face a grim finality, but he will be fed, warm, and out of tragic danger until the end, which, while sad, will be peaceful— much less horrifying than lingering, lonely death from illness of injury, or sudden horror under the wheels of a car.

Don't Suffer

Don't torment yourself over the ones who get away. I've had more than four hundred successes, so you can imagine how many times I've whistled and murmured sweet nothings to a pet who turned and ran away from me.

Checklist

❏ Know you can't catch a dog or cat who really doesn't want to be caught.

❏ Know even stray pets must accept help to get help.

❏ Know you can't help them all, but it matters, if only to you, that you try.

The most important detail is to put your phone number on your pet!
It may save his life almost immediately.

Lesson 10

PROVIDE A SAFE HAVEN

You manage to get back home, with an extra package. You have a dog or cat who's not at all sure what you're up to. Now what?

The first thing you do is secure the pet in its new environment—in the house, the yard, the garage or guest room. Let him get acquainted with what will be his own sleeping area. Feed him immediately. Any place that offers food is likely to be deemed "safe" in a waif's mind. Put out fresh water, and give your guest a while to settle down to his new digs.

The next, and very important, step is to tag the stray. You have accepted responsibility, which requires your making sure the pet's second chance doesn't go sour. If the pet happens to break away from you, someone will find him, read the phone number, call you, and you can continue your good deed. After all, you've made a commitment.

Tagging your stray is healthy for your peace of mind as well. It helps you over that hump of hesitation to the good moment of taking full charge. The pet is yours now and you intend to do right by him. If the pet breaks away from you now, he won't be roaming helplessly anymore. He has a guardian angel. He has you.

It makes no difference to me whether any pet is licensed. That is between you and the state. All I'm concerned with is a *phone number*. Official tags and vet tags are hard to trace. Many people don't know how to track down a pet's owner with only licenses and vet tag numbers. Those are also useless on weekends. A phone number never sleeps, never closes, and never confuses anyone looking at it.

The best identification is the phone number on the pet's collar, in almost any form. A simply flea collar with the phone number written on it in ink is fine. Another simple and instant method is to take a small piece of paper, write your number on it, and use clear tape to wrap it onto the collar. Packaging tape is best.

What's the reason for this? Simple: anybody, anywhere will help a pet with a phone number. People are reluctant to become involved with an unidentified pet, just as you were before you started reading this book. However, an animal with a phone number is an instant known quantity. Somebody has take charge of this pet and will answer the phone. Your pet or your foundling has an excellent chance of being returned to you very quickly if he just wears your phone number. It's simple, cheap, and there's no excuse not to do it.

Tell that to the dozens of people every year who insist *their* pets don't need IDs. Yeah, and bees don't buzz. Insisting your pet is the one who doesn't need to wear a phone number is a sign of plain stubborn stupidity. Dump your ego, grow up and tag your pet.

Now I'm going to tell you something no other author will ever tell you: put this book down and go put a phone number on any animal you have in the house.

Paper, pen, strapping tape. Go!

Any decent owner of any pet, indoors or out, should have his or her pets securely mounted with identification tags. Even my cats wear collars and tags.

I've also had plenty of arguments from people who insist, "*My* dog never gets away from me." "*My* cat lives inside." "*My* pet never leaves the yard."

Really?

I've actually had this argument with a woman while she stood in my yard, retrieving her runaway dog, who had made it all the way through the neighborhood to my house. The woman had the nerve to claim, "Oh, he never gets away from me."

After the fifth time, I indignantly declared, "Well, he's *here*!"

And if I hadn't headed him off, he would've been across town before long. As far as I know, she never did tag the dog. It was some kind of strike against her ego to put a phone number on her pet. Curiously, she didn't find any embarrassment in the fact that she was being *deliberately* irresponsible.

Your pet never gets away from you? Your pet will never be spooked by fireworks or chased by another animal or break away from the kids or be frightened or distracted or jump out of a car door or... or... or...?

Just like the friendly bull terrier who arrived beside my car in my mother's neighborhood, dragging his leash, but without a phone number. I broke my own rule and put a FOUND ad in the paper, because this dog had quite obviously just slipped away from someone's very hand.

Indeed, he had been with his owner during a Fourth of July celebration and been shocked by fireworks exploding overhead. He had bolted, and his owner had lost her grip on the leash.

She was four days searching for him, and had to drive thirty miles to my house to get him. We had a "tag" conversation.

There are hundreds of mishaps which cause good pets to become lost pets. You're a careful driver, but you still carry accident insurance, right? Your children are unlikely to be lost or run away, but you teach them their phone number, don't you? It's also a kind of accident insurance. Your kids can get separated from you in malls, theme parks, even at school. What if something happens to you, and your pet slips away during the turmoil? Isn't it better that he carries his phone number?

Your pet needs a kind of accident insurance too. He needs to wear his phone number. A dog or cat will never be able to speak up and tell anyone his phone number. He has to wear it on a collar. It's a five-minute thing, yet people actively, furiously argue that *their* pets don't *need* to carry ID. I'll never understand what the big deal is or why there's so much resistance to putting a phone number on a pet. Buy a cheap collar and clear-tape the phone number onto the collar. It works.

Checklist

❑ Put your phone number on all of your pets' collars.

❑ Encourage everyone to do the same.

❑ When you bring home a stray, feed and water him immediately.

❑ Put a new arrival in a quiet place where it can sleep.

❑ Relax and go about your normal business.

Lesson 11

SHOULD YOU TRY TO FIND THE OWNER?

The owner of the pet you've picked up obviously didn't bother with a tag. That's dereliction of duty right there. You are not obliged to spend money on lost-and-found advertisements. You are not obliged to canvass your neighborhood or the area where the pet was found. You're not obliged to spread fliers, put up posters or take any inconvenient or expensive measures at all. Those are the responsibility of the person who let the pet become lost without an ID. The onus is on him to take measure to find his pet.

Some newspapers offer "FOUND" ads for free; you may wish to take advantage of that. It's easy and doesn't hurt to announce that you have found this critter.

Your obligation is to keep an eye out for posters, ads and fliers. You may drop your telephone number off at a few neighbors' in the area where the pet was picked up and ask them to phone you if fliers or posters do appear, but you're not obligated to give your personal information or phone number to anyone if you're uncomfortable doing so.

You can also notify local animal shelters, the Humane Society or ASPCA and the animal control department. Let the local network know you have picked up a pet of this description.

However, beyond that, you don't have to disrupt your life. You have not stolen anything; you've done a good deed by picking up this animal. Picking up a pet doesn't mean you have to become a detective to find the irresponsible party who lost him.

Any pet owner knows whether or not he has lost his pet. If he does not put an ad in the newspaper, call local animal shelters, and let it be known that his pet is lost, then he doesn't deserve to get the pet back. This might seem harsh, but I'm hardened after years of picking up after other people's irresponsibility. Everybody knows a pet should wear a collar and ID. If they don't do it, then I guess they're going to learn a hard lesson, aren't they?

You are not a hotel or an animal shelter. It's inconvenient for you to have an extra pet around. You've already gone above the call of duty by sticking your neck out to capture and bring home this lost waif. You have no reason to feel guilty or obligated about finding the person who lost this pet. You also have no obligation to hold onto this pet longer than is comfortable for you. You don't have to wait weeks for the owner to decide to advertise or make some public effort to find his pet.

Wait a reasonable amount of time if it's convenient for you. A week is plenty enough time to get a LOST ad in a newspaper, put up posters, and call local authorities and shelters. If an owner hasn't noticed or bothered to care in that amount of time, then it's truly his loss. All the better reason to tag your own pets and monitor their whereabouts strictly.

Checklist

❑ Load your cell phone with the numbers and names of local animal rescue organizations, shelters, and animal control.

❑ Let the professionals know you have picked up a stray.

❑ Check in with veterinarians' offices for fliers posted by those who have lost a pet.

❑ Knock on a few doors of neighbors—if you feel safe doing so—to see if they recognize the pet.

❑ Give them your phone number in case anyone comes looking for the pet.

❑ Watch your local newspaper for LOST ads.

It's not enough to find a home for a pet; you must find the right home for that particular pet, a match for his size, breed traits, needs and individual personality, or it just won't work out. These are our grown children, Gordon, Lydia and Ben, with a reunion of rescued pets. Photo by Ayaz P. Jafri.

Lesson 12

FIND THE RIGHT HOME

You've decided to recycle this pet to a new home. As this waif's second and probably last chance, you impose an obligation upon yourself to do a good job finding him a new family. He'll have a better second chance, and you'll feel better, if you pay strict attention and do a conscientious job of finding a home, rather than rushing to accept the first offer that pops up. Bother to take the time to find the *right* home, not just any home. Let it take time.

A stray you've picked up is in unfamiliar territory at your house and is probably still looking for its original owners. Dogs and cats are like children; they will be loyal to the worst of parents. The pet will still be trying to get back home, even if home was bad. You must immediately put an ID phone number on your strays. It's even more important for them than a pet who knows where he is.

Tag the cat, too

Cats should also be collared and tagged. There's no reason not to. Even indoor cats should wear identification. How often do we hear of cats "slipping out the door?" If an indoor cat slips out, she's likely to be confused and easily spooked by her surroundings. The outside of a house is much different from the inside. She won't even know where the door is or how to get back in. Your cats, whether indoor, outdoor, or stray visitors, should all wear your phone number.

I've heard all the excuses: "My cat just won't wear a collar." "My cat just falls on the ground and refuses to get up." "My cat has a convulsion if I put a collar on him."

Yeah, yeah. Would you let your kids get away with that kind of tantrum or refusal? Put a collar on the cat and make it tight enough that the cat can't get his paw through it. Walk away. Believe me, he'll get used to it. Sooner or later he'll come out of his conniption and get over his horror at wearing a collar.

Strays are likely to break away from you, and you must remember this: You are the pet's second chance, one with the odds in the pet's favor for a change. Make it a good chance. If he gets away from you, he will soon be back because he'll have your phone number displayed and *anybody will help a pet with a phone number on him.*

Then you can continue helping him instead of wondering whether or not you made his situation worse.

The Gutter Kitty

My children, picking up my precedent, came home one day with a clump of fuzz more or less in the shape of a cat. They'd found this cat running back and forth in the gutter outside our house, going nowhere, but going there mightly fast.

We took this oddball inside and confined it to my daughter's room, which has become the stray-cat hostel. The cat roamed the room in a very eccentric way, bumping face-first into furniture and into us.

The cat was friendly, but weird. We settled down to the houseguest, fed her, and provided litter.

That very evening, my husband scanned the Lost and Found ads and discovered this:

"LOST: BLACK/BROWN LONGHAIRED CAT, 15 YEARS OLD, NEARLY BLIND. NEEDS MEDICATION!"

Obviously gone for at least two days, since there was time to get an ad in the paper, the goofy cat belonged to a woman we know, about two blocks over. Oh, the sobs of relief! This always-indoors, mostly blind cat had somehow slipped out of the house. With all the protests I've heard over the years ringing in my head—*But my pet never gets away from me!*—I urged the happy owner to put her phone number on this cat. Next time would very probably not be so lucky a reunion for an old blind cat.

Ironically, the woman who owned the funny fuzz is one of us—she picks up stray animals even more vigorously than I do, and has been known to stalk and collect kittens out of dumpsters. We had a tag talk.

If the old kitty had just worn a phone number in the first place, she could've been home days before, or at least the moment we found her.

Checklist

❑ Put your phone number on cat collars, too.
❑ If the cat doesn't like wearing a collar, too bad.

Another of Angel's kittens, born to a mother who was still a kitten herself.

Lesson 13

LET THEM TOUGH IT OUT

Wash, groom, and de-flea your stray, or hire a grooming service to do it. The cost is nominal; professional groomers do a good job and can frequently identify problems or injuries you might not notice.

Or just stick him in the bathtub and suds him up. Use regular shampoo if you don't have pet shampoo. Don't use dish soap unless the pet has grease or oil on his coat, although it really won't hurt.

If you have a dog or cat of your own, you will probably already know how your own pet deals with spare animals. I have a simple method—I put my animals together from the get-go and let them tough it out. I don't go through any fancy sniff-under-the-door rituals. With our first cat, Simmony, this was fine. He liked everybody and everything.

With our second cat, a green-eyed ghost of Simmony named Spooky, bringing in other cats is virtually impossible. She doesn't mind dogs, but she absolutely despises other cats and will fight or hide. Generally, animals will set up their own relationships pretty quickly, but if they attack each other, I separate them for the duration. The only time Spooky has ever bitten or clawed one of us was when there was a stray cat or kitten somewhere in the house. Even baby kittens are not tolerated well. If we can keep her from discovering that there are other cats around, we can get away with keeping a guest cat for a couple of days, but that's it. We've had to adjust somewhat to her demands; after all, she lives with us and she deserves some consideration. We've had to lock any cat-guests in our daughter's or son's room until they can be cycled to new homes. It's a little inconvenient, but they just have to deal with it. I'm in charge, not the cat. If Spooky behaves too badly, she gets a swat of discipline.

Yes, you can spank a cat. Yes, you can.

Yes. You *can.*

Give it time

Don't be discouraged if it takes a day or two for your guest to settle down. Dogs frequently bark, and cats don't know the rules. Whatever you do, do not put the guest in his quarters and then ignore him except for feeding. Be sure to interact with him as often as possible. This fosters trust and affection and makes the waif want to please you. Leaving an animal alone only serves to create fear and distrust at a time when an animal needs more socialization, not less. He needs to become at ease with humans, no matter how short the exposure is. Animals can get very quick bad impressions of humans, but also quick good impressions. Even if a stray is only with you a short time, make that time affectionate and comfortable.

Give it a name

I've named every one of my strays from the start. Pets pick up on names fairly quickly, or at least soon get the idea that a certain sound means you're calling them. It also helps you begin

Even pets who are well cared for can break away or be scared into running. Make sure your pets are wearing your phone number!

to see this creature as an individual. Humans regard names as a ticket to intimacy. Friends call each other by first names. Until your waif has a name, he's just a bag of bones and hair. Giving him a name makes him special in your mind and your family's. Our most creative guest-pet name was Rush Limp-Paw. Think about it.

Discipline

Just because you're going to be bringing in foundlings doesn't mean you have to sacrifice the order and tidiness of your personal space. Your home should not be cast into upheaval because of a stray pet's visiting for a while. That pet has to do the adjusting, not your entire household. The stray needs to be taught the rules of your house, because, of course, he has no way of knowing the rules until you impart them to him. Begin right away. I do, whether a stray is with me for a day or a month. Teach your guest the boundaries of living well with humans. No pet is worse off for having learned some manners during his stay with you.

My strays are made to learn basic obedience: down, sit, stay, lie down, don't pull the leash, shut up, and be polite around people and other animals. If they act badly, they get spanked. You would spank an unruly child, wouldn't you? Pets are four-legged children.

Do not be timid. You have to show the stray that you are in charge. Never let anger lead the way. Never kick or use anything but your hand to spank a pet. Impart consistent, firm discipline. Swat when necessary. Do it again the next time, at exactly the same level. Swatting is not beating. No animal—dog, cat, child, or otherwise—will be traumatized by being spanked for bad behavior. You won't have to call the pet therapist.

Many "experts" claim you shouldn't use your hand to discipline a pet because that's the hand that also loves and feeds them. Ridiculous. If a pet learns that your hand is the instrument of control *and* of affection and food, he will learn to tell the difference between his behaviors, and not your hand and something else you use to spank him. He'll only learn to hate the thing you use to discipline him.

Dogs and cats aren't that stupid. They perfectly well understand the connection between something they do and the reaction it causes. Higher-intelligence mammals like dogs and cats are capable of learning rather large vocabularies of human words; they can certainly learn to do and not do a thing based upon what your hand does, and they know your hand is attached to you.

By the way, you're not allowed to hold a grudge. You are allowed to *only* be angry for the amount of time it takes to handle the immediate bad behavior and the discipline for it. Snarling at a pet all day or withholding affection only confuses the animal. They don't lodge things away for future grumbling the way we do.

In fact, it's important that you forgive him relatively soon. This proves to the pet that *this* behavior is the bad thing, and not his very existence. Pet who have been undisciplined or beaten for no reason can't tell the difference.

You may identify a particular behavior problem and try to deal with it. For instance, a cat may incline to scratch furniture. Swat him or scare him away, then immediately provide something he *can* scratch, such as a scratching post or a piece of old carpet nailed to wood. If a dog is hand-shy or leash-shy, work on this by the hour and by the day. Be consistent. Use the same tone of voice every time. Be cheerful and friendly, but firm. Dogs react well to repeated rituals, especially if there's something pleasant involved, like a walk or play in the yard.

While *Dog Whisperer* Cesar Millan may or may not agree with everything said here, he is right that dogs live in the "now" and can be taught new behavior, no matter their ages or their pasts. Consistency, firmness, calmness, affection and emotional balance work well with both dogs and cats. Watch his show. Good stuff.

Checklist

❑ Be consistent with training. Establish boundaries and stick to them.

❑ Discipline and reward with your hand.

❑ Be firm, but act quickly.

❑ Never be abusive and never remain angry after the problem has been addressed.

❑ Never hold a grudge or anger any longer than it takes to reprimand a pet.

Lesson 14

CATS CAN BE DISCIPLINED, TOO

*C*ats can't be disciplined. Where did such an absurd idea come from? A rumor spread by cats, probably.

What are we afraid of? Being snubbed by a cat? *Really*.

"My cat runs the house." When your cat pays the bills, he can run the house. Let's get over this one right now. Think about how cats treat each other. They definitely discipline each other with physical action and tone of voice. *Hissss—whack*. Yes, you can swat a cat.

Cats respond well to repeated kindness, firmness and consistency also. They're usually quite smart and understand boundaries in both territory and behavior. They swat each other as a method of discipline, and they understand what it means. Chasing cats with a feather or squirting them with water are just silly. What does a feather or water say to a cat? They understand your hand, both in discipline and kindness. I've had multiple dozens of cats in my stray-plucking career, and every one has responded just find to disciplinary swatting, even new ones. The idea that you can't spank a cat is a complete myth.

I once visited a home with several dogs and a cat. The wife refused to discipline the pets because she was afraid they'd have some kind of stroke or turn against their owners or some other complete nonsense, and the husband catered to this. They would swat the furniture, stomp the carpet, use spray bottles of water—anything but spank the pet. As a result, their pets were out of control, irreverent and misbehaved. Late one evening, I sat down to dinner, alone in the dining room, only to find a hound under each arm and a cat walking toward me straight down the middle of the dining table.

Two swats and a backhand took care of all three.

Though these were somebody else's rude pets and had never been disciplined in their lives, they never bothered me again. Lo and behold, the ill-mannered dogs and cat learned very quickly to stay away from the place where the people eat. They didn't have any traumas, episodes, strokes or panic attacks. They didn't hide from me or have a hissy. No cat has any business on a kitchen counter or dinner table. We wouldn't allow your children to behave this way, so why on earth would we allow our pets to do it?

None—and I mean none—of my cats ever goes on the table or counters. My cats also don't jump up on the couch or chairs, on our bed, or on any of my guests' laps. They're not allowed and they know it. You just have to let your animals *know it* and leave no doubt about exactly which behavior has caused the spanking.

Don't scream, rant, turn violent or throw fits. Never spank an animal with a stick or even a rolled up newspaper. Simply secure the pet (hold onto him), give a good swat in a sensitive area, and say, "No!"

Next time, do it again, the same way. Do I actually have to say *don't cause injury or severe pain*? All right, consider it said. We're not here to advocate abusive behavior by two-leggers any

Kittens born to stray cats become feral very quickly and are difficult to socialize. If you know of stray kittens, get them off the streets immediately, before their personalities harden against human companionship.

more than bad manners from pets.

Cats understand, as do dogs, being brought back to the scene of a crime and being swatted for what they know is their own work. They have sound memories and remember scratching or peeing in the wrong place. The area also will hold the cat's own scent, and she will recognize it. She'll know she was there and not to go there again the way she did before. Whether it was scratching a couch or walking on the kitchen counter, she will learn. Cats are not stupid and they won't have traumas if they get discipline. Look at any cat disciplining another cat. Do that.

I don't recommend training with food treats. If you gave your child a piece of candy each time he used good manners, you'd soon have a monster on your hands. Dogs and cats are the same. Reward the animal with vigorous loving touches and a happy voice of congratulations.

Train your stray with very simple and consistent methods. Remember that the family who adopts your foundling will probably not have taken any training courses or know any fancy methods. Just do what makes sense, then tell them what you did and encourage them to keep working on the same behaviors.

And please don't call a psychic!

Checklist

❏ Correct unwanted behaviors by not permitting them.

❏ Give a firm swat and a strong "No" everytime a correction is needed.

❏ Be confident that cats can be taught what not to do.

Cyber, a purebred German shepherd who had been badly neglected, with her new pet boy, Thomas DesRosiers. Cyber lived a very long life with her adoptive family. More about Cyber in Lesson 20.

Lesson 15

IT'S OKAY TO LOVE THEM

You already have a big heart, that's clear. Picking up and recycling animals to new homes can be somewhat of an assault and battery on the emotions. Don't worry about it; it only proves you're the right person for this hobby. You'll eventually develop a thicker skin and learn to impart affection without making a commitment in your heart and mind that comes to pain at separation.

My philosophy is this: Go ahead and love them. You'll do a better job finding a new home because you'll care where they go. You must give them up, simply because you need to make room for the next one who comes along. If you don't send them to new homes, then you'll either have to stop helping other strays or you'll be overrun by them. Neither of those is a good option.

My husband has been strict with me. One dog, one cat, and all the strays I want to help, as long as I keep the general population down to one dog and one cat. So far, so good. I never fool myself that the stray I just picked up will be the last one I'll ever see. Greg's one-and-one rule has worked well. There's

There are many more kinds of domesticated animals that need homes, other than just dogs and cats.

always room for one more.

Go ahead and fall in love. You'll be a stronger advocate.

What if the kids get attached?

Children always get attached to animals. It's a fact of life and love. Don't even try to stop it. Don't separate your kids from your foundlings. Let them interact and learn to like and appreciate each other. Generally, it's emotionally healthy.

Do explain the nature of what you're doing to your children, that you're all helping this new pet on his way to a better life. He won't be running lost in the road anymore. He needs a new family and it's up to all of you to find one.

Despite adult misgivings, kids understand temporary relationships. There's a certain reality about not being able to keep every pet that wanders through your life. I have raised three very loving and pet-oriented children through my four hundred strays, and the result has been excellent. My children have grown up with the idea of helping animals who need help, and have begun to capture and bring home strays on their own, which we tackle as a family responsibility. My daughter's room is the Motel 6 for stray cats, our elder son is responsible for the dogs, and the younger son is the chief affection-giver. Together they have succeeded in caring for and socializing several animals that might not otherwise have been adoptable because they were not well enough accustomed to human companionship. They have all learned to successfully and joyfully say goodbye.

One way to ease separation anxiety is to check on the animals a few weeks or months down the line. The stories usually have happy endings, and often we will visit our foundlings in their new homes. This gives the kids a tremendous sense of success at the value of their efforts and sacrifices.

You're glad to give your children shelter, financial security, and all the wonderful things good parents can provide. Take this as an opportunity to give them a priceless gift of the heart: love for animals and a strong sense of self-control.

Checklist

❏ Love them; you'll find them a good home.
❏ Get the entire family involved.

Young Dundee in our back yard in Flint, Michigan. Fortunately, he lived in the house with us and was not banished to the yard, as too many dogs are. Dogs and cats should sleep in the house, with their families.

Lesson 16

DUNDEE AND THE SPOOK

I'm not an advocate of getting pets for other people as a "surprise." It's no better a bet than redecorating a living room while the owners are away. In fact, it's worse. A pet is just not a life decision anyone should make for anyone else.

Yet that's how I got one of the best dogs around.

At eleven years old, our wonderful Sharvan was at the vet's for her yearly shot, when the vet discovered a leathery growth inside her mouth on her lower jaw. The terrible revelation was melanoma. Sharvan had cancer.

We immediately had the growth removed, but further tests disclosed another large tumor on her heart. She was terminally ill. We were devastated. Loving a pet is very much like loving a child. A pet is a child who never grows up, no matter how old he or she gets. You spend your time, trouble and resources caring for and loving this creature, and someday, though you're still caring and loving, the pet's time comes. A life winds down.

Sharvan was still vital and active at eleven and we weren't

ready or prepared for the idea of losing her. Our young family was about to suffer a terrible blow.

She grew steadily weaker over the next few months, despite a costly operation with money we really couldn't afford to lose. She spent most of her time lying exhausted under the Victorian square grand piano in our little dining room. The situation grew quickly more hopeless. We finally made that critical decision to end her suffering, once we knew she really was suffering. The decision to euthanize someone you adore, to end the life of someone who trusted us completely to protect and defend her, is as agonizing as watching the suffering.

As heart-wrenching as this is, I wish human beings would have the courage and wisdom to do for each other what we know is decent and best for our beloved pets.

We called for help—a close friend of ours from Dearborn, Tony, dropped everything and drove up to Flint just to help us through the terrible day. He went with us to the vet's and stood by us. Sharvan had a peaceful passing.

We brought Sharvan back home, curled on my lap almost like a puppy. She seemed smaller somehow, lying across my legs. We intended to bury her in my parents' back yard, next to our greatly loved miniature poodle, Suzette, whom I also miss to this day. I feared explaining Sharvan's loss to our son, who at the time was only two years old. In fact, Gordon got the idea and dealt with what came. He touched her and understood that she was gone. We got through it.

Tony, we discovered, had detoured on his trip from Dearborn and picked up a pet coffin, something which we didn't even know existed. He worked feverishly to dig a grave in the hard ground of my folks' back yard, and Sharvan was laid to rest.

A few days later, I was in our dining room, which in our small house also served as my writing desk, when I noticed Simmony the cat sitting in Sharvan's place under the grand piano. As soon as my eyes contacted his, he let out his plaintive broken meow.

"Ah—ow?"

Like something out of a Lassie movie, I knew exactly what he was asking almost as if he had spoken actual words. *"Where is she?"*

I said, "Aw, Sim... I don't know how to explain to you that she's not coming back... "

I've written millions of words during my career, and would give them all to have been able to speak to Simmony just for thirty seconds. It had been far easier to explain to two-year-old Gordon.

Three weeks went by. We invited Tony and his wife Wendy to come for a more pleasant occasion, to thank them for their support. They were two hours late, but eventually their car arrived.

And at Tony's heel loped a goofy red spindle with two big brown eyes that seemed to ride right on the top of its nobby head. They had brought us a dog.

Uh-oh.

What could we say? "Sorry, but we're just not ready." "Sorry, but we haven't even adjusted to Sharvan's death yet." "Sorry, but we'd like to pick our own dog when the time is right." "Sorry, but we're not in a mood to train a puppy right now." "Get that mutt the heck back in your car, clown."

None of those seemed quite appropriate.

And this was one goof of a dog. He was six months old, red as a penny and all legs. He had long hair except on his ears, and was some kind of Irish setter/golden/somebody mix. And he nipped. And he was incorrigible. And he ran off. And he was untrained. And his entire brain could fit in the little knot on the top of his head. And, and, and...

Well, he was housebroken, so that was something. That's all he was. The rest was completely uncultured.

I stuck a pin in a map of Scotland and named the dingdong dog Dundee. Greg promptly nicknamed him "Dumb-dee." This gangly male turkey was klutzy, had none of Sharvan's elegance, and didn't even have the sense to have long hair on his ears like a setter is supposed to. He would run in figure-eights around our backyard like a lunatic, and didn't have the brains to know he could've jumped our little fence any time he wanted to. I guess that was a good thing, but it proved this was not the brightest bulb in the box.

Dundee, Tony and Wendy said, had actually been with them for nearly two weeks. They had found him at an animal shelter. He had been adopted twice and rejected both times for being "incorrigible." In other words, he bit, barked, and ran.

When they adopted him, he was one day from euthanasia.

Did we want a dog so soon after Sharvan? Could we actually put this goofball in the same league as our charming and elegant flat-coat? Could we ever love him half as much?

Could we look at our friends, who had executed what they thought was a wonderful gesture, and reject the gift?

What a situation.

Well, rather than make a rash decision, we let the dorky dog hang out in our household while we thought about this.

There's something to the idea that animals have more common sense in some situations than people do. While writing at my computer in the kitchen nook about a week later, I happened to notice Dundee sitting outside on the old rug we'd put in the yard for him. And who was curled up next to him...? Simmony the cat.

Simmony had no reason whatsoever to go into the backyard. He could've completely ignored the strange dog. He never bothered to go back there to sit with any of the stray dogs. Did he sense that something was different?

In his innocent wisdom, Simmony was communicating quite

clearly to us that life without a dog was just not normal for us. He missed Sharvan, and we had magically begun to fill that hole by providing *him* with another friend. Out of the mouths of... well, you get the idea.

Dundee stayed. We simply trained him to be a polite boy, not to nip, and not to run away. Whomever had twice rejected him apparently were not very well-trained people. I've discovered that to be the more common truth—it's usually the people who are badly trained, and not the poor pet who is sent to a shelter because he hasn't learned enough.

Dundee never attained Sharvan's level of elegance and beauty, but he did grow into a healthy, strong and good-looking setter mix the color of autumn maple leaves. Our children grew up with him, and he turned out to be a sweet and dependable companion for us and for Simmony.

White-Faced Simmony lived to be eighteen years old, still catching birds into his last days. He grew deaf, however, and did not hear the car that struck him one September day.

We were inconsolable. Simmony had been with us through all our ups and downs, all the stray animals coming and going, all the successes and failures, through three children and all our memories together. He was our little anchor, the little man in our lives who never changed and was always there, no matter what else happened. Losing him was a shock, in a very strange and unexpected way. We knew he was very old, yet he was still like a child, a fixture in our lives, a white shape in our window, and it's hard to let a child go when you're still taking care of him.

Now it was poor Dundee's turn to be confused.

We lauded Simmony's life with the best tribute we knew to offer—providing a home for another homeless cat. At our local Humane Society we discovered many kittens, and I was determined not to have another all-white cat. I couldn't stand the grief. We held and played with every kitten in the place, except the all-white one in the cage in the corner.

Diane's mother, Susan Carey, a 90-year cat hater, was won over by the family's second permanent cat, the Spook.

At the last minute, I reached to the cage in the corner and stuck my finger through the mesh. The white kitten began licking my finger.

Oh, what the heck. I pulled out the fourteen-week-old American shorthaired white and turned her upside down in my arms, the way I used to hold Simmony. She took to it, clasped my hand between her paws and began licking my fingers vigorously.

That little pink tongue got the white kitten a home. We brought the white kitten home and put her on Dundee's face.

"Here's the new one. Get used to each other."

The white kitten went through several names for the first few days, until I noticed she curled her periscope tail the same way Simmony did. In my periphery, I thought she was Simmony, until I remembered he was gone. Despite being half his size, she was like Simmony's ghost. The Spook was here to stay.

Dundee has lived a privileged life somewhere near the center of attention. He became slower and stiffer with time, but thanks to modern veterinary care and daily arthritis medicine, we still take a long walk every night. He makes it quite clear to us when it is time for the walk. Spooky doesn't follow us on our walks as Simmony did, but she does wait for us in the neighbor's yard and stalk our return. She twists upside down and rolls in front of us to show her pleasure that we were back. She has climbed onto my desk while I was writing, and often slept with our youngest son. We were a complete family again, with a dumb but big-hearted setter and a cat with no pride who completely adored us. Through them, Sharvan and Simmony remain still part of our lives.

Who can ask for more?

Checklist

❑ Never surprise anyone with a pet.

❑ If you lose a pet, let yourself grieve, but another will emerge. Love just gets bigger.

❑ Each pet is different, so don't look for a substitute.

❑ Train people right and the pet will be trained correctly, too.

Carefully select the kind of animal you might like to foster, then do it methodically and with prior study of that species.

Lesson 17

OUT OF SIGHT, OUT OF MIND

"Free to a good home" really translates as *Free to anybody who'll take this problem off my hands.*

Nobody responds to such an ad by saying, "Well, we're not a very good home for a pet, but give it to us anyway."

No one who advertises this actually bothers to ask a question or two about what kind of home this will be, good or otherwise. This horrible practice is most common with kittens, but also happens with unwanted puppies. When irresponsible pet owners carelessly let these kittens and puppies come into the world, they want to be rid of them—the sooner the better. Any home qualifies, good or bad or otherwise. They don't care. Out of sight is out of mind. The kittens and puppies are not given proper early-life inoculations, are not spayed or neutered, and are often just another in a set of litters that keeps happening to these people because they don't spay or neuter their adult pets.

No, "any home" is not necessarily "a good home." There are myriad true horror stories about unscrupulous laboratories, hunting dog or fighting dog training, and other vicious, heartless scoundrels scooping up whole litters of kittens and puppies from *Free* ads and signs, then using these puppies and kittens for experiments or arena bait. Good home?

Never, never, never give an animal away free! Never give an animal away without asking the questions suggested in this book. If you're inclined to do this kind of thing or are that anxious to get rid of a pet, then be honorable and grown-up: take the pet to a shelter and pay the surrendering fee. They'll make sure the pet gets necessary medical attention, is spayed or neutered, and they will be strict about what kind of new owner gets the pet.

Checklist

❏ Never, ever, give a pet away without checking the adopter's background.

❏ Never, ever advertise "free" pets or "free to a good home."

❏ Encourage people with unwanted kittens or puppies to take them to a shelter, or give them this book and let them learn how to find new homes the right way.

❏ Encourage them to SPAY their cat!

Lesson 18

CHARGE AN ADOPTION FEE

Why charge money? It reduces your chances of finding instant homes for your pets, yes, and people who don't have much money won't incline to come to you.

Well, that's the idea. After the last chapter, you know the problems with many "instant homes." Don't be in a hurry.

Why charge a fee? Well, first of all, you've put some expense into this enterprise and might as well replace some of the money. If you're recycling a stray, then you've provided safe harbor and you deserve to have your investment covered.

Second, anyone who cannot fork up a few dollars to adopt a family pet will also not be able to afford food and veterinary care for that pet. Very simple. Pets are never really free. It costs to have pets, just as it costs to have children. People who cannot afford pets or kids should simply not have them.

In a world of **FREE** signs, where everything else costs something but animals' lives are considered valueless, you're

Fostering tiny kittens and puppies takes its own kind of patience and expense, but is very rewarding. Spay or neuter all young pets before finding them homes. Many shelters or vets have discount services.

liable to come up against some resistance. When people balk about your charging money, here's what you say:

"Free things are seldom valued. This pet deserves to go to a home where he is of value. The fee also helps pay for food for the next one I help."

Any decent wannabe pet owner will appreciate this. No free pets, ever.

How Much Should I Charge?

This is completely subjective. A fee as low as fifteen dollars may be enough to cover the expense of the ad and encourage the prospective owner to value his new friend. The fee may also depend upon the pet's breed, desirability and disposition, and any number of other factors. A full-blooded German shepherd may command a higher fee than a mixed-breed mutt. You'll have to experiment and gain experience.

Some people who rescue and recycle pets become very strict about the new homes. Such people and organizations like rescue centers will spend considerable time, effort and money making a dog or cat healthy and secure, then spay or neuter the pet and pass that fee along to the new owner. This brings the adoption cost up, but many people are willing to pay for a pet that has already been spayed or neutered. If you find yourself doing this on a regular basis and building a good relationship with a vet, then spaying or neutering is an excellent guarantee that you won't be contributing to your own problem by cycling your foundling to someone who lets him/her procreate.

If you don't want to have your foundlings spayed or neutered, there are ways to find homes that will do that job. More on that later.

As a general template for an adoption fee, add up the cost of two weeks' worth of pet food, the advertisement you publish, and add five or ten dollars. The total will probably range between twenty-five and fifty bucks. Start there. After all, you're not in business to make money. You want to cover your expenses and make sure the people who adopt your pet are making a real commitment and have the resources to continue caring for him. People who want bait for a fighting dog ring will not pay anything for dogs and cats. It's too easy to get free ones.

Legally and financially a dog or cat is a possession, a commodity, as is any property. They command a certain dollar figure, and that figure is largely subject to market and other forces. Later we'll discuss a process for weeding out the bad and seeking out the good, but for now we're talking about money.

Some people rescue only dogs or cats of certain breeds. Purebred dogs or mixed breeds of desirable breeds tend to command higher fees on the recycling market. With experience, you'll come to know which types of pets command higher fees.

You can also contact certain rescue services for particular breeds. For instance, sound out the Internet by putting "Labrador rescue" or "Irish setter rescue" or "Siamese cat rescue" into a search engine. Then contact these people and ask their advice on finding a new home for your guest. They'll already have an idea about the market for their preferred breed.

Veterinary offices are also great sources of ferreting rescue centers because they often work closely with them. The vets and folks who work them are almost always pet enthusiasts and can be very plugged in locally to the pet adoption and rescue scene.

In every case, you should charge something for an animal you have rescued, some amount which you will use as a barometer for weeding out the people who cannot or will not assign dollar value to what is really a very important investment and commitment.

Checklist

❑ Never give a pet away for free.

❑ Don't feel guilty about charging a fee; it's the best way to make certain the adopters have the commitment and resources to care for a pet.

Lesson 19

THE TRAGEDY OF TOO MANY

Millions—that's *millions*—of healthy dogs and cats must be destroyed every year in America simply because they are unwanted. There aren't enough homes. We are creating far too many puppies and kittens. One unspayed female creates multiple babies with each pregnancy, and if just one or two of those females go unspayed, the number increases exponentially. The number of "barn cats" alone is mind-boggling.

Facts about U.S. Animal Shelters

According to the American Society for Prevention of Cruelty to Animals, ASPCA, there are about five thousand community animal shelters nationwide that are independent that have no direct national government oversight. There is no national organization monitoring these shelters. The terms "Humane Society" and "SPCA" are generic. Shelters using those names are not part of the ASPCA or the Humane Society of the United States. Here are some telling statistics from the ASPCA's website:

Approximately five million to seven million companion

animals enter animal shelters nationwide every year, and approximately three million to four million are euthanized; that's about sixty percent of dogs and seventy percent of cats. Shelter intakes are about evenly divided between those animals relinquished by owners and those picked up by animal control. These are national estimates; the percentage of euthanasia may vary from state to state.

According to the National Council on Pet Population Study and Policy, less than two percent of lost cats and only fifteen to twenty percent of lost dogs are returned to their owners. Most of the lucky ones were identified with tags, tattoos or microchips.

Twenty-five percent of dogs who enter local shelters are purebred, accord to Pet Population statistics.

Only ten percent of the animals received by shelters have been spayed or neutered, while the vast majority of cats and dogs pets have been, according to the American Pet Products Association.

The bottom line is lost dogs and cats typically are never found and most that wind up in shelters are euthanized.

Angel's story

The evening was new and cool. The small city around me was just closing for the night. I was walking home from my daughter's house, three blocks from my own. We lived on the same street, but the night was so fresh that instead of going straight down the street, I decided to make the walk longer and go around the block to the next street over.

Halfway home I noticed a car parked with its door open and a man leaning into the car, illuminated only by an interior light, and a slight glow from the streetlight at the end of the block. Suddenly a white form dashed from under the car, or behind the car. I couldn't tell.

The man looked around at the form. It was a cat. The cat

crouched in the middle of the street and looked back at the man. Then the cat dashed for the dark bushes across from where the car was parked.

I said something—I don't remember what—some kind of friendly comment, I guess. The man didn't respond, but got in his car, started it up and drove past me quickly, then rolled around the corner behind me and disappeared.

I paused and looked back that way, trying to understand what I'd just seen. The cat hadn't come from under the car or behind the car. That man had just booted the cat out of the car. The lowlife was dumping his pet.

Other than maybe child abuse and neglect, there's nothing lower than cruelty to animals. Among the lowest, laziest, most rotten-hearted humans are the ones who dump their pets. They took on this responsibility, but rather than manning up and doing the right things, they dump their pets into the unkind world, assuming somebody else will take up their burdens. They have no care for the pet, who is frightened, confused and endangered, left by the side of the road, wondering where his master is and when he will come back. I've seen the look in these pets' eyes. It's almost human.

I've encountered this kind of thing before; once on our way up north to our cottage, I spotted a black-and-white cat on the shoulder of the road, looking dead. But as we were passing, the cat raised her head and looked at me—her nose was bloodied and she had obviously been thrown out the window of a moving car. She was blinking and stunned, barely able to move. Her nose had been smashed on the concrete and was badly scraped.

Of course, we picked her up, so her fortunes improved. We took her with us to the cottage where, sadly, she soon gave birth to two stillborn kittens, still in their amniotic sacs, grown enough for me to see their beautiful markings. They looked just like her.

We found that cat a new home, but I think often of the two kittens, so close to birth, whose lives were ended because some swine tossed their little mama out the car window because she was pregnant. These are the same swine who didn't bother to have the cat spayed when they should have.

How often does this happen? If you know someone who has a female cat, pester him or her to get the cat spayed. Call him the names he should be called if he doesn't bother to do it: lazy lowlifes who shove their responsibilities onto others and contribute to the misery in this world. It's unforgivable and inhuman.

The white cat that dashed into the bushes disappeared. I called, "Kitty, kitty," for a few minutes, but really didn't have much expectation. I went home, haunted by what I had seen. Finally I got a can of cat food and went back around the block to look for the cat. I hoped maybe she would smell the food, but no luck. Eventually I had to just go home.

Two nights later my daughter was just closing her front door when she noticed a cat sitting right there on her porch.

"Well, hello," she said. "Who are you?"

She already had two cats and didn't want another, but having been raised in our house and having experience with strays, she took the cat in for the night.

The next morning I received a phone call from my somewhat flustered daughter. "She's having kittens!"

Well, I knew Lydia didn't have experience with this, so I quickly went to her house in time to assist in the birth of two more kittens from the street kitty, who in the light of day wasn't white, but a cream-colored tiger. The mother cat was only about seven months old and extremely friendly. All she wanted was cuddling. She paid no attention to the three newborn kittens because she didn't know what they were. She was too young for those instincts to have kicked in. She shouldn't have been pregnant at all, being barely more than a kitten herself.

Lydia went to get a box and a towel while I pushed a baby kitten up to the mother's nipples and tried to show her what these little creatures were. Then I heard a little squeak that was unaccounted for. When Lydia returned, I told her that I'd heard something. She hunted under the bed, and sure enough there was a fourth kitten deposited there in the dark by the confused little mama.

Lydia named the sweet mother Angel, because she really was an angel. The foul vipers who had dumped this cat were missing out on one of the sweetest pets around. Angel quickly learned what her babies were and became a devoted mother. Lydia rose to the task and raised the four kittens. There were two that looked just like Angel—cream-colored with pale tiger markings, and two who must have looked like their father—white with gray-black markings.

Rather than being born under a porch or in a bush somewhere, probably to die of malnutrition when Angel went hungry after being dumped, the kittens were raised with love and affection. This meant they became well-adjusted "people cats," and the best kind of pet. When the time came, Lydia found two homes for them, each willing to take two of the kittens. She is still in touch with their owners, and the cats are fat and happy together.

Lydia adopted Angel, who was just too adorable to give up. In time, one of her other cats died of natural causes, so Lydia was back to two cats, generally regarded as a household limit. At the age of seven, Angel was diagnosed with kidney disease. Lydia tackled this by learning to give the cat subcutaneous fluid treatments. While Angel will have a shorter life than most cats, she is doing well in the care of her own guardian angel—Lydia, the young lady who took the responsibility and who has received the rewards of loving the sweet young mama cat who was kicked out of a car, but ended up on the right front porch.

Checklist

❏ After spaying your cat, badger the neighbors to spay theirs.

Lesson 20

THE CASE FOR MUTTS

Mixed-breed dogs and cats are frequently healthier, longer-lived, less delicate, less finicky, less skittish, and smarter than purebreds. Any geneticist will tell you that life is meant to mix and is stronger when it does. Mixed-breed dogs and cats may not be as sophisticated or impressive as a papered or purebred animal, but the genetic advantages of strength, smarts, toughness and resistance to illness are worth considering. Open your mind, go to you local humane organization or animal control agency, and give a home to a smarter, tougher pet who will be with you a long time and not bring big vet bills which frequently accompany purebred lineage.

The Problem with Purebreds

Yeah, I know you're out there. You read *Old Yeller*, and in spite of the brutal ending you've always wanted a purebred golden retriever or yellow Lab. Your grandmother had a Tonkinese cat and you've held out for one. You live in a small apartment and know only a schnauzer is right for you.

Highfalutin' breeders will churn out litters of puppies and kittens, claiming *their* animals are okay to proliferate because they're papered, pedigreed, better, higher, expensive, valuable, pure... pick your adjective.

Fine. *But...* every puppy or kitten born, statistically, puts at least one other on the death row. In America we are forced to euthanize—kill—nearly ten million unwanted pets yearly, perfectly healthy and good dogs and cats who must be killed simply because there's not room for them in our domestic world. They're certainly not all mutts. Whether they are mixed breeds or not, they're certainly not all "bad." In fact, the enormous majority of them are wonderful, friendly, trainable pets who, though no fault of their own, fall into the hands of the wrong people or wrong situation, or both. Even pedigrees end up dumped, pregnant, roaming, surrendered, abandoned or otherwise without owners.

Much of this misery is created by people who simply want to augment their incomes by having their own purebred pets produce puppies and kittens which can then be sold. Whether these people running puppy mills know it or not—and they usually don't care—they are contributing to a long line of misery stretching out into the unforeseeable future

Yes, I'm painting with a broad brush. I know that many people who breed pets are responsible and caring. However, from my point of view—that of someone who picks up the unwanted pets—there are just too many dogs and cats being born. It is my hope that breeders have their pets reproduce less often and allow more animals to find homes.

Not all the people who purchase purebred pups and kittens will be responsible pet owners, and unwanted breedings will happen. The numbers are mindboggling and fast-growing from just one female, and, of course, many of those offspring will be females.

Humans naturally assume that a more expensive "product" is better. We assume this because it's frequently true.

In pets, however, it is not necessarily true. Not all breeders are responsible. The world of purebred pets is fraught with corruption. Some breeder pets are so inbred that they come out with health problems which can translate into big vet bills, shorter lives, and eccentric personalities. Mixed-breed dogs and cats can be physically hardier, less high-strung, less finicky and longer-lived than hybrid pets. Again, a broad brush, and I'm not a vet or a scientist, but it's worth researching before you commit to a purebred pet.

I believe it's also a myth that your female pet is better off having one litter before she's spayed. There is no medical evidence supporting this idea, and my personal experience is the opposite. All my female pets have been spayed before having litters, and they all turned out fine. Please don't create more babies to add to an already huge overpopulation just because of a myth. Check with your vet before you let your pet breed. Then spay, spay, spay, neuter, neuter, neuter.

If your real desire is to have a purebred pet, yet you still want to help chisel down the roster of homeless dogs and cats in the world, there's an excellent way to do this. The Internet.

There are four greatest inventions of all time: the printing press, the flush toilet, the automobile, and the personal computer. The modern communication wonder of our time, the Internet, allows us to mingle ideas, resources, needs and wants on a level never before available to us. We are a great species to have come to this (thank you, Bill Gates and all other heroic entrepreneurs.)

If your fondest desire is to have a purebred Irish setter, all you need do is log onto any search engine and type in "Irish setter rescue." The Internet will lead you to a farm of choices from kennel clubs to organizations which specialize in rescuing Irish setters from any imaginable situation which has left them homeless.

There are also organizations which specialize in placing "hard to place" pets. Our good friend and fellow author Dave Galanter adopted a deaf kitten and his hearing littermate, the latter of which was just unwanted. There are pets which are missing a leg or have one eye, or have been through desperate situations such as fires, which left them unattractive. They are often excellent pets because they've been through such hardship that they're endlessly grateful and happy to be warm, fed, and loved.

Many greyhounds need homes after their racing careers are over, startlingly early in a dog's life. One fortunate pet lover found a purebred poodle at the dog pound, a lovely and affectionate debutante who had been thrown away because she didn't match her owner's new furniture.

Therefore, hunt around before you spend hundreds of dollars supporting the breeding industry. You may just find a cheap treasure that desperately needs you. And remember: every pet is a champion. Bloodlines are just window dressing.If you want a purebred pet, consider getting one that doesn't have papers.

Purebred animals are fine if that's what you want. However, be aware that they often come with health problems endemic to each specific breed, often because of inbreeding. We were devastated by Sharvan's early death because of melanoma. Flat-coats, we later discovered, commonly get melanoma before living out their full lifespans. The good news is that a vaccine has been developed that may mitigate this deadly problem and has been conditionally approved by the U.S. Department of Agriculture. This scientific solution is good to hear because flat-coats are among the most wonderful of family dogs because of their happy dispositions and gentle nature.

Before spending hundreds of dollars on a breeder puppy, try

to contact one of the many breed-specific rescue organizations for your particular breed. It's as simple as putting the breed plus the word "rescue" into a search engine like Petfinder. It's that simple. You'll find yourself linked up to services that specialize in finding homes for purebred pets who have no homes. How much easier can it be?

Also consider that an older pet might be right for the situation you have. A two, three, or five-year-old pet might be more settled, housebroken, and easier to deal with than a young pet, and they make perfect companions for single people, older people, or families that don't want to deal with young pet requirements or training.

Cyber's story

A wealthy family in our neighborhood had a beautiful full-blooded and papered German shepherd, the real German kind, not the more familiar Americanized shepherd. This female dog had a magnificently sculpted head, was smoky black with some tan markings and was quite large and elegant, but almost never in good health. She was friendly, but very shy. Too shy, really. When I first saw the dog, I thought she was over ten years old. She was only two, barely out of puppyhood, but her hindquarters were hollow and bony because she didn't eat well. She looked like half a dog. The owners tried to feed her, but never bothered to change her food or discover why she had no motivation to eat.

An injury turned up on one leg and the open wound wasn't healing. The dog's eyes were dull, her demeanor sullen, and she seemed weak all the time. Now, try to line this up with another fact: the father in this family was a *doctor*. Yes, a real medical doctor, and so were his brothers and father. And, no, I still can't figure this out.

Ultimately the couple wanted to move back to New York City, so the doctor took the dog to the big city while the wife and children stayed in Michigan as they set up a new life in

Cyber was living with the wrong people and was unforgivably neglected. We talked them into giving her up, nursed her back to health and adopted out to a wonderful family with whom she lived a long life.

Metropolis. Greg and I had business and a wedding to attend in New York. While there, we stayed with the doctor and the dog, during which the dog's sad situation was revealed to us.

The dog was being ignored. Though the doctor was kind to Cyber, he didn't have time or wouldn't take time to properly attend his pet. Cyber was forced to urinate in the very small apartment because she was rarely taken outside or walked at all. She slept in a small cage and ate very little. She became even more emaciated and weak. Her leg wound was still open and sore.

Seizing the moment, I took Cyber out to the nearby park and slowly began exercising her. After an hour or so, she began to limber up and trot with me, though sluggishly. Her eyes brightened somewhat.

We returned to Michigan, leaving Cyber with her owner in New York, but knowing she was not being treated well. I spoke to the wife, who was anxious to get rid of the pets her husband seemed to accumulate, including another dog and some birds. While the husband was in New York, the other animals disappeared to—well, I'm not sure where.

One day the wife called and said, "He's here with a truck for the furniture, and he's got the dog with him! Come over!"

Greg and I went immediately and spent until midnight helping them load up their furniture in a rental truck. Cyber was tied to a doorknob the whole time.

When we finished, and they were about to drive away, heading back to New York, I said, "I'm leaving now. And I want to take Cyber with me."

The doctor was reluctant—he really did like the dog, but he didn't have a clue of how to be a good dog owner. The two have to go together. Liking animals is not enough. Some people should just not have pets.

Saying I would keep Cyber at my house and give her some exercise while they got settled in New York, I took advantage of a moment of transition when the doctor had so much else on his mind. Cyber came home with us.

Over the next few days, Cyber continually broke away from us, hobbled around the block and tried to get back into her former house, which was empty. Dogs are loyal even to bad owners, and she didn't understand why her family was gone and she couldn't get in the house. It was heartbreaking to see her peeking inside the windows. She was a better pet than they were pet owners. Luckily, she was tagged with our phone number, so anyone who found her could call us immediately.

For the next several weeks, we tended her leg wound and took her for a long walk every night. The walks were magical. She began to cheer up and get stronger.

We mixed more appetizing food for Cyber, and since she was getting exercise she began to eat with more and more vigor by the day. Her hind quarters filled out and she started to look like a whole dog.

The New York family still had relatives in Michigan and came back for a visit during one of my kids' birthday parties. Cyber was understandably excited to see them. She thought they were coming to get her. The family was amazed at her good condition. Their young son even asked, "Is she eating?"

I said, "Oh, yes, she eats and exercises here."

Then I took Cyber to the backyard so they wouldn't get any ideas. I would never have given her back to them. Rather than say that, I simply separated them.

Cyber grew stronger and, miraculously, younger. Her coat turned less bristly, her eyes brightened, and she started acting like a young shepherd. She took a liking to me and would follow me around the house and sleep in my office while I worked. She stayed near me whenever she could. That gave me a hint about what kind of home she would need.

I phoned some close friends who had moved to Kentucky. That family comprised of a woman quite a bit like me, an attentive dad, and a little boy who was an only child. They had several cats, but something was missing. I told them about Cyber and suggested that she was the right match for them and their son.

Well, they ruminated over this for a few days and surprised us with a call. They were coming to meet Cyber.

The family spent a weekend with us and seemed only passively interested in the dog. I thought I might have made a mistake. That would be fine; no one is obliged to take a pet he or she isn't ready for. I never pressure people into taking animals into their homes. There's always a home out there. I might have to spend a little more time finding Cyber's new family.

But to my pleasant surprise, just before they left the mother asked her son Tommy if he wanted to take Cyber home, and he said he did. I knew Cyber would be in excellent hands.

And she was. I received reports of Cyber's good health and happiness, her contented owners, and the happy walks to the local arboretum. Though Cyber tried to remain loyal to her original owners, as dogs will, the best place for her was a new family and a new life.

Checklist

❑ Give mixed breeds a chance.

❑ If you're set on a purebred, look for one online through a breed-specific rescue group.

❑ Consider getting a purebred that doesn't have papers. They need homes too.

❑ Consider an adult or older pet. They can be great matches for older folks.

❑ Make sure bigger dogs have a yard or get plenty of exercise.

❑ If you're set on a purebred, do your homework. Some breeds are prone to medical ailments.

❑ Spay or neuter your pet. There are too many dogs and cats and not enough homes.

A very young Angel, with her newborn kittens, one day after being thrown out of a car.

Lesson 20

WHEN YOUR PET HAS BABIES

If your own pet has babies, it's not your pet's fault; it's yours. When you need to find homes for them, you can use the template in this book to do it. And, I'll exclaim it again; *Please do not give baby animals away free!* You've already used bad judgment and been careless in letting your pet become pregnant. Don't compound the irresponsible act by shirking your full responsibility to these little creatures you've let come into the world.

Your obligation is to let these young animals nurse their mother and be together as a family for at least 8 weeks, preferably 10 or 12. It makes a difference in their lifetime behavior, sociability and general health. You must subject them to lots of human touching and interaction, so they'll be well adjusted to human companionship.

After you've done your job for these weeks, find homes for these young creatures and charge money for each one of them.

Don't burden your friends or relatives

Don't pressure your family, friends and acquaintances to take pets they aren't ready for. They'll get the idea that you find homes for animals and tell you when they're in the market for a new pet owner. If they're not, they won't want to see you coming.

Let your friends know you're not going to be badgering them to take foundling pets off your hands. All this is part of not feeling desperate to *get rid* of a creature you're temporarily housing. If you're prepared to deal with boarding a temporary guest, you won't feel burdened and your friends won't hide when they spot you. You don't need to foist pets on unwilling homes. There are homes out there who want pets. Your job: find them.

If your pet or stray has babies, settle down. The parent will do most of the work. Your job is to find them a comfortable, somewhat secluded place where they feel safe and are comfortable, a place where they can make a mess without destroying your home or room.

Accept that you will have the pups or kittens for seven to eight weeks. The newborns need that much time with their littermates and parents to be physically and emotionally strong and well-adjusted enough to make it on their own with a new family.

If you cannot make a full commitment to keep the mother and babies together for the needed amount of time, or you're simply unable or unwilling to take on the task, find a reputable rescue group or shelter. Check with a local Humane Society chapter for suggestions and contacts.

Offer to send along some pet food or cash to help shelter or rescue family feed the animals and care for them. It's the right and polite thing to do.

Finally, if you stick it out, speak with a vet about what to do and what to expect during the birthing. If you can't handle it alone, find an experienced pet handler to help you. Mother pets often can give birth on their own, but some need help, especially first-time mothers. Get prepared. There's plenty of information online about what to do. Call a veterinarian for advice, as well.

Checklist

❏ Research what to expect during the birthing process, or call a veterinarian.

❏ If you have the puppies or kittens, be prepared to keep then seven to eight weeks.

❏ If you must hand off the pregnant pet, ask a rescue group to help place it.

❏ Give a donation of food or money to those who take on the pet.

Lesson 22

HOW TO FIND THE NEW HOME

If you pick up a stray pet, the question rings through your mind: *Should I go ahead and find a home for this stray? After all, he's somebody's pet...*

Keep this in mind: You are this stray pet's second chance and probably his last chance. Remember the lesson of the road? If the pet's owner were paying attention, the pet wouldn't be roaming the road. Of course, some pets do slip away, but why was this pet roaming without an ID on his collar?

Relax

You've decided to recycle this pet to a new home. As this waif's second and probably last chance, you impose an obligation upon yourself to do a good job finding a new family for him. He'll have a better second chance, and you'll feel better if you pay attention, are strict and do a conscientious job of finding a home, rather than rushing to accept the first offer that pops up. Bother to take the time to find the *right* home, not just any home. Let it take time.

Take a deep breath and relax. There is a home out there to match this pet. The process may take days, or even weeks, a few ads, a little longer and so on, but patience and persistence will pay off. Don't feel pressured into handing your helpless guest over to the first caller. You're not a Wal-Mart.

Where to place an ad

While many conventional newspapers are shrinking or disappearing, a local newspaper is still a good medium for an ad when you're ready to cycle your foundling to what the rescue community has come to call a *forever home*. There's a great responsibility in those two little words—they mean a great deal. They mean that the next home for this pet should be the home for life, where he is loved, played with, touched, nurtured, given a place to sleep inside the house with the family, and is given good veterinary care for the rest of his life.

Newspapers are fine and can be effective in getting the word out about your pet's availability, age, and a few key facts.

The second most effective medium for an ad is *Craigslist*. This is a very fast way to get responses and targets geographic areas. On Craigslist, you can post photos and offer a longer description of your pet and his traits and needs. It's also free, while newspaper ads usually carry some fee.

And certainly there is always *Petfinder.com*, where you can list your foundling, describe him and his medical condition, his needs and his history. You can also post several photos, and that always helps.

Newspapers, Craigslist and Petfinder.com are better for ads than, say, a bulletin board in a grocery store, because the bulletin board can lend itself to spontaneous decisions or instant gratification—you know, whimsy. People who are seriously looking for a pet and have been thinking about getting one are more prepared and more likely to be good permanent homes than somebody who just sees a pet's cute face and is swept up in the moment. More serious people tend to actively search

Never, never stand in a parking lot or at a fair with a sign on the pet that he is available to adopt. Again, this leads to snap decisions that can't be corrected later, and you really don't know where your pet is going. After bothering to capture him, house, feed, nurture and otherwise help him, you deserve to know that your little buddy is going to a permanent new home with people who have thought about getting a pet, considered all the ramifications and prepared, not just somebody passing by who are taken up with his big brown eyes.

How to write an ad

People looking at PETS FOR SALE ads are actively searching for a new pet. They want one and they're ready to pay. They've thought about this and they're receptive. They're the people you want to speak to. Go right to them: take out an ad.

Before you call the newspaper, decide what your ad will say. Keep it short, because a three-line ad costs less than a five or seven-line ad, and you may have to run a second one. Be honest, and upbeat.

Here's the formula for composing an ad:

Breed, color, sex, age

Something nice about the pet

Needs family, or needs second chance

Phone number

So the ad will look like this:

> **Lab mix, black and brown neutered male, about 2 years. Shy, but loves kids. Pepper needs family. 333-444-5555.**

> **Beagle mix, brown/white, male, one year. Playful and loving. Housetrained, healthy. Samson needs a second chance. 333-444-5555.**

Orange cat, female, five years. Loves to cuddle; one-owner would be best. Pumpkin needs you. Call 333-444-5555

Let the ad run for three days. Although most newspapers give breaks on ads that run for a week or ten days, I've found that it's unnecessary to run an ad that long. Usually there are responses within the first week, sometimes even the first day. You end up spending more than necessary by running long.

Don't forget to put an ad on Craigslist and Petfinder.com. These are very easy to use, take photos, which always help, and can run for longer than a newspaper ad. Craigslist allows for a much longer ad, more details, mutiple photos, history of the pet as you know it, why you're circulating him to a new home, descriptions of his personality and good/bad habits, medical details and how much training you think he might require. The more information, the better.

No response?

If there's no response on your ad, wait a few days, then rewrite the ad or change or expand your advertising area to include a larger range or different town. Usually just waiting a week and revising the ad slightly does the trick.

Be patient. You've just started.

When someone calls

This is the point at which you must become somewhat stronger and more firm than you might incline to be.

"You have a dog for sale?"

Remember, you are not obliged to hand over your pet to the first caller. Don't be intimidated. You are the advocate of a helpless life. You have to do this firmly and well.

The person will ask a few questions about the pet, probably just repeating the ad. "Age is about two? He's friendly? Likes children?"

Then, he or she will probably ask, "Why are you getting rid of him?"

Whether the caller asks or not, you should offer up the information:

"I find homes for pets who don't have homes. He was abandoned and running on the street. His owner never showed up. We've made sure he's healthy and now he's ready for a second chance."

The caller will ask, "Where do you live?" or "Can I come over?"

This is your point of challenge.

People think that putting an ad in the paper means you're handing them a free ticket to come look at this pet and that they have some right to come over. They don't.

You should say:

"Well, hold on a second, please. I'm this pet's last chance, so I have some questions to ask, if you don't mind."

If they mind, then you hang up. Most people don't mind at all. Good pet owner prospects never have a problem with this part. It's your first signal about the person you're speaking to. Does the person like or dislike the fact that you're being fussy? A good home for the pet will like the idea and answer eagerly.

Have you ever had a pet before?

If the answer is, "No," then ask:

Why do you want a pet now? Are you ready for such a long-term commitment?

A college kid or someone renting a house or an apartment is

not acceptable. These are people whose futures are unstable. The pet needs a permanent situation with grown-ups in charge—and that doesn't refer to the age of the person.

If the caller has had pets before, ask:

How long did the pet live?

If the answer is, "He was about three," that's not enough. Why don't they have him anymore if he was only three years old? Simply ask that. *What happened?*

There aren't many good answers, but you'll learn to tell the difference. "He lives with my uncle on their farm," is probably okay, and much better than "He ran away."

If he ran away, why didn't they search for him and why wasn't he tagged? I've come to the opinion that there are very few good reasons to fail getting back a pet you've lost, as long as he's tagged and you make a good hardy search with newspapers, posters, and checking shelters regularly. Far too many people lose pets and never get them back because they were careless in the first place, then don't bother to make a good search. They should not be given another pet.

If the answer is "Ten years," you know you're on the right track. Acceptable answers for animals kept just a short time are things like "He got cancer."

Unacceptable answers are: "He ran away." "I gave him away." "We moved." "Somebody stole him," "He got sick and died," "It got hit by a car." "I took him to the Pound/Humane Society."

To those types of answers, your reply is:

"Sorry, but a pet is a living thing and a lifetime commitment. You didn't take good enough care of your previous pet. I won't give you mine."

Yes, you should learn to be that brutally honest. You are the pet's second and last chance. If he gave his pet away, lost him or her, surrendered him or her to a facility, of some other unnatural folly, you boldly say, "Sorry, but I have no way to know you won't do the same to this one."

The person calling will be angry and insulted. So what? Don't be afraid to say this kind of thing; more people need to hear it. Be bold and strong. It's part of the commitment you've made, and it will make you a better person.

If initial answers were acceptable, then probe deeper.

Where did the dog sleep?

The only really acceptable answer is "In the house."

Unacceptable answers are: "Out in the yard." "In the garage.' "There's a pen outside." "We've got a doghouse." "In the barn."

Dogs who sleep outside are usually ignored. That's a cruel but common fact. Few people actually go outside and spend the time every day with a pet, which is really required by living, breathing social animals like dogs and cats. Dogs and cats are pack animals. They are family-oriented. The owner and his family is the pet's pack. A dog or cat doesn't understand being forced to sleep away from the pack. They become unsociable and often psychotic. Dogs bark at everything, hoping to get some attention, and cats simply become unfriendly and solitary. It's very sad.

Your answer is: "Sorry, but dogs/cats are social animals and should sleep in the house with their pack members. They don't understand being alone, and they shouldn't be. A dog/cat is a living creature who needs interaction with a family."

They'll be insulted. So what? They'll also hear something they need to hear.

Your next question is: *Was your pet spayed or neutered?*

The acceptable answer is:"Oh, yes, I wouldn't have it any other way."

Unacceptable answers are: "No." "She had five litters before we spayed her." "I want her to have one litter before we spay her." "I just can't do that to a male." "They're just following instincts." "God, I'm crossing my legs already!"

Anyone who doesn't spay or neuter pets is contributing to a horrific problem in our world. He's the jerk who creates unwanted pets, and you're the kind soul who takes up the burden. Don't contribute to your own problem. *Never* give a pet away to a person who doesn't have the right attitude about spaying and neutering. Period.

Your answer is: "Dogs and cats are not humans. They have physical urges, not sex lives. He won't miss his pearls of nature. Millions of unwanted dogs and cats are put to death every year because there are too many puppies and kittens being born. I don't want to add to my own problem, or allow more misery in this world. I'm working against that. You're obviously not. Thanks for calling."

Checklist

❏ Use local newspapers, Petfinder.com or Craigslist to place ads.

❏ Get vital information in the ad in three lines or less.

❏ Post pictures if you can.

❏ Advertise the pet as "for sale."

❏ Again, never offer a pet for free.

❏ Have screening questions ready for those who inquire. Write them down ahead of time so you don't forget.

❏ Don't be afraid to ask tough questions.

❏ Don't be afraid to say no.

Yes, dogs can be "fine" outside with good shelter and insulation, but they are emotionally starved and lonely. Their personalities will be warped by lack of human contact.

Lesson 23

NO OUTDOOR DOGS

ERIC'S STORY

One of the big warning signs during home-finding phone calls are these statements: "I want a watchdog," or "Our dogs always live outside." These are red flags for me.

Outdoor dogs are eventually left lonely and ignored even by owners with the best of intentions. People live busy lives and sooner or later, the dog will be ignored. It just happens.

I know what I'm talking about; when I was in my early teens, we accepted a German shepherd puppy from neighbors, a young black male whom we named Eric. He was a beautiful puppy and he lived out in our garage. My father was an Arkansas country boy and figured the dog was "fine" outside.

Well, if "alive" is "fine," then Eric was "fine." He was also very lonely and ignored. He had a large yard to run in, but that didn't replace companionship. When winter came, our time outside became shorter and shorter as the fascination of having a pet faded away. Cold weather drove us inside and Eric was left outside. He had shelter in our garage, but no personal warmth. Before long, his entire exposure to the family who had adopted him was a cracked-open back door and a can of dog food spilled on the step.

I get shudders now just thinking about it. Imagine every day just dumping food on the step and closing the door. Poor Eric!

Eventually Eric began barking at the neighbors over the fence and grew more eccentric with time. He became less and less sociable. This was not his fault. How could he be sociable if he had no practice? Anyone, human or otherwise, who spends all his time alone will turn into an eccentric and intolerant individual. We see this every day with people who live alone or gradually withdraw from society. Sooner or later, it's just not healthy.

Eventually Eric grew nervous around people and took a nip at a neighborhood child. My parents, not knowing how to deal with this, decided to get rid of him. As a budding teenager, I had no power. My parents just didn't have the skills or the inclination to care about Eric or make sure he had a good future. Their decision to find him a better home was in their interest, not his.

Today, as an adult, I would never abandon a pet this way. Eric turned into a nipper because we had made him that way. As is so often the case with people who don't accept the full breadth of their responsibility, our dog would pay the price for our failures.

We took him to the Leader Dogs for the Blind facility in Rochester, Michigan, but Eric was head-shy and not social enough to make it past the first test. He was frightened and skittish, of course, since he had never been anywhere but our backyard and had never been around other people. None of this was Eric's fault. It was our fault. We had been poor pet owners.

One of the workers, though, said he knew a place where

Eric might be welcomed, possibly a farm. My last sight of my beloved dog—and I did love him—was this magnificent, large, elegant German shepherd huddling inside a gated cubicle, with his ears down and his chin lowered, and his eyes sagging in fear. He looked small and terrified. And we walked away. Out of sight, out of mind.

Well, out of my parents' minds. But I cried. I was the only one in our family who thought of him, missed him, or who still thinks of him. He was a good dog with a pleasant temperament but was not neutered. I have never forgotten nor quite retired the sense of guilt. I remember too many times putting my hand out the cracked-open door with the can of food I was dumping on the snow-covered step. All these years, I've remembered his sad face at that last moment in the kennel. Imagine the situation from Eric's point of view. He had done his best and was being abandoned in a cold blue box by the people he trusted.

My parents were relieved of their responsibility for Eric and didn't think about him again. They also didn't think about the pain and anguish suffered by their daughter: me. How often do parents ignore a pet or get rid of a pet without thinking about the effect on their children? Children see pets as other children, members of the family. What is the lesson to our children when we dump a pet out of our lives? The result is children who get a sad look at what their parents are made of, and how little their parents value a helpless child. If you want to give your children one of the best lessons in life that you can, just be kind, responsible and custodial about your pet. Don't abandon his needs any more than you would abandon your child's. Your child will notice.

We don't know what became of Eric. My parents never checked. Whatever happened to him was our fault, not his. No dog should be an all-the-time-outside dog. Dogs, big or small, belong inside with their people. We've already discussed the safety factor—your dog is a much better guardian for you when he lives inside, when he regards you as his pack, his family, and not just the can-openers he glimpses now and then. Outdoor dogs become pathological, maladjusted and unsociable, and will frequently bark at anything, anytime, all the time.

Also, burglars case their targets and know which dogs are outside all the time, leaving the inside of the house vulnerable. On the other hand, no burglar will put his foot into a house with a dog living inside and risk being bitten. Burglars are generally lazy, trying to get something without legitimately working for it, and there are easier targets down the street.

People have gotten the idea that a dog is a cheap way to guard a yard. In fact, outside dogs do not make good guardians. If you want an outdoor burglar alarm, buy an outdoor burglar alarm.

Dogs are "family" animals. They're affectionate, they form relationships, they love and they're loyal. How can they love and be loyal to people they hardly see? If your dog lives in the house with his "pack" members, he will be much more inclined to protect. If you want a devoted protector, bring the dog in.

Dogs who are outdoors all the time also tend to see the people in the house as puppies hiding in a cave. Seeing themselves as the top of a hierarchy, they can become aloof and overprotective in a bad way, and thus may even turn dangerous.

Dogs who live inside come to see themselves as members of the family and the people as seniors of the pack. They will be better adjusted, better balanced, and have the right sense of "pack order." They will have the right idea about human beings and will take orders much more willingly.

Burglars know all this. They know people stop looking outside when the outside dog barks, because outside dogs bark all the time at nothing in particular. Why pay attention?

Burglars also know that if the dog is outside, then there's *not* a dog inside. As the daughter of a county sheriff's lieutenant, I learned that burglars usually "case" a neighborhood before choosing a house to break into. They learn a family's habits and take note of important things, like whether this family has a dog inside the house.

You want real security?

Bring your dog inside, neighbor.

Checklist

❏ Dogs are pack animals and should live inside, with the rest
of the pack. Period.

Our son Gordon, at 15 years old, walks our newly adopted Cairo, our aging Dundee, and beagle Lady Bug, adopted by our friend Dave Robertson, at this writing a Michigan State Senator. Photo by the Argus-Press, Owosso, MI.

Lesson 24

MAKE THE BEST MATCH

When people come to your home, you'll get a very good idea quickly about what kind of people they are. If they're happy and physical with the pet and he likes them, you'll be able to tell.

Don't be afraid to say no even at this point! Have the nerve to say, *Maybe this won't work out. I'm sorry,* if you get any bad vibes or if the people really don't seem to know how to handle the pet. You do not have to surrender your pet just because the people came over.

Good signs are such as bringing children, smiling and laughing, vigorous physical contact with the pet, and a sense of confidence with the pet. Most of us know what that looks like. We've seen it on *Lassie.*

Remember, you are under *zero* obligation to hand over your foundling to anybody, any time. If your instincts tell you to say no, then the phrase is, "I'm sorry, but this isn't working out. I'll be keeping Bobby for now."

So they're mad. So what?

However, odds are good that the situation will work out if you've done your telephone screening job properly, patiently and courageously. If you remain calm, assertive and in control, by the time someone actually comes to your home, you should already know it's going to work out.

The Bad Match

One example of disaster in matching a pet to a home is the Disney "Dalmatian" movie phenomenon. Every time Disney puts out a spin-off of *101 Dalmatians*, there's a rush on Dalmatian puppies. A few months later, a shocking number of these grown-up Dalmatians flood back into the rescue system because the personality of a Dalmatian is drastically different from the movie version. While they fit in well with people who understand the breed, Dalmatians are not without their demanding traits. Anyone who wants one, or any breed, should research that breed thoroughly and talk to people who own them or foster them.

A neighbor of ours adopted a dog after seeing the dog's picture in a Humane Society ad. Her son liked the dog's face, and they adopted him even though he was a basset hound mix. They had a small house with an even smaller yard with no fence, and the dog was untrained. The woman was a single mother with a quiet voice who had her hands full, and suddenly they had a not-very-bright field dog that was completely wrong for their situation. The dog tended to jump up, barked too much, ran off uncontrollably and forgot to come back, and was completely brainless about cars. He was a young, high-energy dog who required exercise, and never got it because he was too strong for the boys to take on a leash. Therefore he was even more frustrated and barky, and tended to break away for a run whenever anyone approached the front door.

The woman and her children didn't have the time, experience or even the physical strength to leash-train or exercise a hound-type dog. They had never had such a breed before, and were clueless. Soon after adopting this dog, the woman married a gentleman who came to resent having to walk a dog whom no one else in the family could manage. The unfortunate result was that they had to find the dog another home, with a fenced yard and some room to run. The dog was confused, the kids were disappointed and the parents were so burned out that now the family has no pet at all.

The irony of all this was that I had offered to give them advice about finding the right dog for their household before they adopted this hound, but the woman never took me up on it. If someone with experience offers advice about certain breeds, shut up and listen! You don't have to take the advice, but at least you will have heard it.

Senior citizens are probably ill-advised to adopt young or very energetic pets, although this of course depends upon the person. Another of our neighbors, at the age of eighty-one, adopted a young Scottish border collie. The dog was vibrant, very strong, and needed exercise—much more than little slow walks with an elderly lady who could barely control her. Desperate for action, this sweet, high-energy dog ran off whenever the gate or door cracked open. While they loved each other and the dog is now over well ten years old, the border collie has lived her life in a small fenced area beside the house, without the exercise critical for her breed. Border collies are bred to run, and they need to run. Our elderly friend would've done much better to adopt a smaller, older dog which would get more out of slow walks. This wonderful lady is now in her nineties and has suffered a slight stroke, but fortunately still lives in her house. The border collie is lucky that her owner lived so long, but certainly has not gotten the exercise she needed, nor a big enough yard area even to stretch her legs. There was a lot of love in this situation, but, with apologies to John Lennon, love is not all you need. Love is never all you need.

However, the situation would've been perfect for an older,

more settled Chihuahua, poodle, or other small breed rescued from a puppy mill who needed a warm bed and some quiet love. There are certainly plenty of older pets in desperate need of homes.

Sadly, most mismatched dogs don't end up with good endings. I have no idea where the basset hound went or whether he will stay in that home, though I hope the situation is better-fit to a hound's sporty personality. Hounds are different from setters, which are different from terriers, which are different from poodles, which are different from shepherds, which are different from Jack Russells, which are different from... well, you name it. The entire situation would have been averted if only they'd done a little research and chosen a breed, age, size, and type which already fit the situation of their household.

It's also a false assumption to believe that a small dog fits better into a house or apartment situation than a large dog. How many fans of *Frasier* have eagerly brought Jack Russell terriers into their homes because Eddie was so darned cute on the TV show? The dog on the TV show was firmly trained, so much so that he paid absolutely no attention to anyone but his trainer on the set. Jack Russell terriers, like all terriers, can be headstrong, dominant, clever and sometimes defiant. Those who wish to own one must thoroughly research the habits and characteristics of the breed, then talk to people who own and foster them.

Many small-dog breeds are fussy, nippy, yippy, uppity and demanding. On the other hand, I've know people who had big dogs in apartments and did very well because larger dogs often tend to be more settled in a house, and are often less likely to nip or be insecure. The only important variable is that larger dogs need vigorous exercise, and not just walking. They need to run or actively play at least once a day, and that is a big commitment that lasts for ten years. My large dogs have always done very well inside, even with babies, kids, and other dogs and cats coming and going, and we are scrupulous about making sure they get exercise commensurate with their needs every day without fail.

Large dogs also have large defecations, therefore anyone who adopts a large breed must be prepared to deal with and dispose of big piles.

Checklist

❏ Research breeds to learn their traits.

❏ Match family traits with pet breed traits, and specific traits of that particular animal.

❏ Seek advice from those familiar with a breed you're interested in.

❏ Have a place for dogs to exercise.

Dogs and cats will adjust to each other and learn to get along.

Lesson 25

BIG DOGS FIT INSIDE

So there is no happiness with three Irish wolfhounds in one small house?

Tell that to our neighbor back on Cadillac Street in Flint, who happily lived with her three giants, the tallest dogs in the world, all of whom slept inside. These monstrous yet wonderful dogs were not a problem inside. Irish wolfhounds tend to settle down, be calm, and manage very well.

Outside, it's a different story; these people owned a typical house for that neighborhood, with a typically-sized yard. The yard was most definitely not big enough for one, never mind three, Irish wolfhounds. They simply needed more exercise than a relatively small suburban yard could provide, and of course they filled the yard and destroyed the grass with feces. Big dogs make big poop, and you had better be ready for that. It's big, it smells, it destroys grass, and it most certainly does not dissolve in the weather. If Irish wolfhounds or any big breed, or multiple dogs of any breed, are right for you, then buy a big property. You'll all be happier.

Get a dog by personality, not by size, then adjust your life to fit that dog. Small dog breeds actually tend to be more skittish, nippy and protective than bigger dogs. Of course, this is not speaking of individuals, but breeds are groups with certain inbred personality types.

Big dogs tend to be calm, less intimidated by people, and often friendlier—again, speaking very generally. Large dogs also tend to settle down inside a house much better than small dogs, and much more than people assume. I placed a dog which most of us would consider medium-sized, a mixed breed with some shepherd, some beagle, and other pals in the stew, with a family that was looking for a small dog because their house was not roomy. I did something I rarely do—I pressured them to come meet this dog, because his *personality* was right for them. He was puppylike, very friendly, nonagressive, and completely loving. I called him Sparky.

I discovered Sparky while looking for another stray who had streaked away from me. This sweet dog was sitting passively in a school yard, watching every car that drove by with desperate attention. He had obviously been dropped out of a car, and was determined to wait until his thoughtless and piggish owners to come back for him. This kind of innocent and noble loyalty is common in pets; when abandoned, they look for and pine for their undeserving owners. A pet that is thrown away will commonly wait in one area for those who did the throwing. The owners couldn't have been good or even kind to the pet, yet the pet will steadfastly wait, just as our Simmony waited outside the Dawn Donuts, and Sparky waited on the school grounds. So sad.

Even as I approached the gentle dog at the school, he continued to scan traffic for his owners. Finding him a new home, and an excellent one which I occasionally visit, was a victory. Sparky turned out to be "the best dog we've ever had" for

Feral cats may never adjust to life with a human family, but there are ways to help them even if they must life wild, which is a short and harsh life.

his new family, more than a match for a rambunctious little boy and his smart sister, and a loving replacement for their previous dog that had just died.

Personality, not size.

Exercise

When finding a home for a pet or finding a pet for your home, remember that different sizes and breeds of dog need different degrees of exercise. Be prepared to provide that exercise, and that means for the rest of the dog's life, and that means at least ten years. Don't lie to yourself and don't assume the kids or anybody else will exercise your dog, unless you pay for a dog-walking service. Don't get a high-energy dog because you *hope* it'll make you go outside and walk or run. If you don't already walk or run regularly, don't get a dog that needs to walk or run regularly.

Check breeds. Some small or medium-sized dogs, like Scottish border collies, need tremendous amounts of daily running, while there may be larger or older dogs that do not actually require much exercise. Smaller dogs may take up less space or use less distance to get enough exercise, but they may still require daily vigorous movement that you may not be ready to provide. Younger dogs need more exercise than older dogs. Do your homework both when finding a home for a dog or when searching for a dog for your home. Investigate the breed, then investigate the specific individual animal.

When finding a home for a dog, do your research into that breed or mix. Then be scrupulously honest when doing your phone interviewing of potential owners. Don't be in a hurry, and don't hand the dog over to a home that may not be prepared for or have a history of experience to provide the right amount of exercise for that dog. If it's a bad match, it's a bad match. Don't follow through.

Checklist

❏ Research the level of exercise a dog needs; some require much more than others.

❏ If you want a big dog, get a big yard.

❏ Match personality, not necessarily size.

❏ Match potential owners with breeds that fit their lifestyles.

Lesson 26

HELPING FERAL DOGS AND CATS

Some domesticated pets do end up feral, which means wild. In America, those who remain feral are usually cats. In other countries, feral dogs are common to a tragic level, even considered a food source and treated quite brutally. If you feel about this as most of us do, consider making a regular donation to organizations in other countries that work for humane treatment or animal rescue.

In the U.S., many feral cats manage to survive in urban, rural and coastal environs, though usually only with the aid of humans. But—and you knew there was one—sooner or later reality catches up to them in the form of weather, accidents, disease, insects, infection, or pregnancy. They need help with all these contingencies. In many states or provinces, the cruel North American winter weather prevents feral cats from having a very decent life at all.

Barn Cats

Allow me to take a moment here to break into the idea of "barn cats." I am a medium-sized city and small-town girl, always have been, but my Arkansas grandmother was pretty sure there was a country girl in there somewhere. She was right. I always had an affinity for country life. I wore cowboy boots and denim, rode horses and even toyed with the idea of owning a stable of show horses some day. Though that never happened, there's a bit of the back pasture in this gal yet.

As such, I understand the concept of letting cats or dogs live outside on a farm, as long as they have each other and warm shelter. Always remember that both cats and dogs are bred to need human companionship. They're hard-wired genetically to need our company. No cat or dog should live a solitary life without companionship nor ever be banished from intimate contact with the people in his or her life. If people don't want to touch and speak to a dog or cat every single day, they should not get pets in the first place.

Puppies and kittens are adorable, but they grow up into adults who are frequently ignored when the cute wears off. Dogs and cats are social animals, each descending from pack animals that lived very closely integrated lives in family environments.

"Barn cats" are often untended, or only fed. Feeding is not enough. Cats must have veterinary care, even if only once a year. They need vaccinations from feline disease, treatment against fleas and other parasites, and most of all to be prevented from having more and more kittens to add to an already appalling number of untended and unwanted cats.

I strongly encourage everyone to *spay or neuter all barn cats*. Please take responsibility and encourage others to do so. Show your disapproval for this kind of human blindness to a very big problem. Farms shouldn't be breeding grounds for unwanted pets when we have simple and cheap ways to stop it. Barn cats are not feral and shouldn't be treated that way.

Feral Cats

What about feral animals? How can we help them? Should we even try?

Sometime within the past million years, *Homo sapiens*

began inviting canines and felines into their caves, their lives, their mythologies. As we humans began to domesticate animals for our own benefit, we discovered that canines—usually friendly young wolves mellowed to the good life and brought to the heel of man—made excellent guardians for our children and our flocks. We began deliberately breeding these canines for certain favorable characteristics, eventually turning them from wolves to dogs. This took thousands upon thousands of years, reaching back into the earliest dim corners of human trivial life. It cannot be reversed.

Cats are the same. In early human civilization, creatures like the saber-toothed cat and other early predatory felines were respected for their elegance and efficiency in the hunt, which early man found almost magical. Large cats were soon troweled into mythology as mankind developed tribal culture and religion to control it. Cats were among the earliest creatures to be taken for gods. That didn't stop us from selectively breeding them down to the familiar housecat we know today. We worshipped them right into our homes, and that's where they should be.

Dogs are not wolves. Cats are not lions. They are domesticated animals who have been deliberately bred, by us, to accommodate life with human beings. As a species, we have an obligation to them.

This is not the same as any charity we may feel toward other wild animals. Various species have always gone extinct and will always continue to go extinct, with or without human involvement. If we contribute to that extinction, we should attend that problem as best we can. That doesn't mean we can always succeed. We have succeeded in many cases, such as the American alligator, the bald eagle and the California condor. We're doing better with tigers and pandas, although pandas are absolutely determined to go extinct whether we like it or not. They only eat one thing, they don't breed, and if they do breed, the young commonly just don't live. We may not be able to succeed with such species as the African elephant, which requires such a wide roaming range that they will always come into conflict with the expansion of humanity.

Humanity has a right to expand, just as any other creature has had its time to flourish. We are hardly the first species to push others out of history. We are the first, however, to try to do something about it.

The Ice Cat

A nose laid open down to the bone, infected. Fur falling off. Too weak to hunt in the late fall chill.

This was the sight that greeted our friends Mike and Gayle in their back yard one day. The pathetic knot of fur and blood was a male cat, so feral that he would not come to them or even eat the food they put out if they were in sight. They put the food out hoping only to offer the black cat some comfort in what were clearly his last few days.

Because Mike and Gayle had a good track record with their own cats' health and with helping homeless cats, their vet trusted them enough to give them antibiotics for "Black Kitty." Amazingly, Black Kitty didn't die, and his nose began to heal.

Because Black Kitty wouldn't allow anyone to come near enough to touch him, Mike and Gayle built him a warm outside box shelter with a birdbath heater inside. The cat slept not in the box, but on the ground next to the box.

Well, one day in the frigid cold of winter, Mike went outside to find Black Kitty lying on the ground beside the garage, frozen stiff under six inches of newly fallen snow. Dismayed, Mike nudged the body, just to confirm the obvious.

Black Kitty had other ideas. The cat suddenly got up, shook off the snow, and looked up as if to say, "Well? Did you bring me any food?"

Surviving his half-feral life, Black Kitty began sleeping under the dryer vent. Still very feral and not allowing Mike or Gayle to touch him, Black Kitty didn't realize that the dryer vented warm, moist air which actually froze when the dryer turned off. The ice caked over him, freezing him to the driveway. Mike took the opportunity and tried to touch him, but Black Kitty cracked out of the ice and skittered away, leaving many tufts of fur behind.

Two more months went by before Mike could touch the cat, who quickly found out that he *liked* being touched after all. However, he never allowed himself to be brought into the house, but remained an outside kitty, weather and all. For three more years Black Kitty stayed with Mike and Gayle, never wanting to go inside even in the coldest of Michigan winter months.

One spring, Black Kitty disappeared. Mike and Gayle assumed he had been hit by a car or maybe taken by one of the coyotes newly brought back into the Michigan ecosystem. But then, late in the summer, Black Kitty showed up under the hedge, asking again, "Where's my food?"

For the remainder of that summer and fall, Black Kitty stayed with Mike and Gayle, then, one day, simply disappeared for good. He is greatly missed, but there's some comfort in knowing that he had three more years than feral life was going to offer, thanks to two people who didn't give up on the Great Ice Cat of the North.

Checklist

❏ Give pets companionship, even if they choose to live outside.

❏ All pets, even outside dwellers, need veterinary care and vaccinations.

❏ Have all pets spayed or neutered, even outside dwellers. Some rescuers capture, spay or neuter, then release.

❏ Remember that all cats and dogs are social creatures, even those that act aloof.

Cats sometimes seem aloof or the same as other cats, but actually have very distinct individual personalities.

Lesson 27

Humans: The Only Animals Who
Care About Other Animals

We argue daily about such environmental issues as the rain forests, which are being cut down at an alarming rate. Should they be saved? Of course. The planet needs them. They are our great atmospheric scrub brushes. They clean the planet. A jungle is what grows if you cut down a rain forest. They're different.

On the other hand, though it's easy and politically correct to say, *Save the Rain Forest!* there are thousands of people whose survival depends upon being able to use that land for something other than wild overgrowth. Given the choice between feeding your children and letting some wild frogs and snakes live out their lives, which would you select? These people have a limited world view, are worried about this life here and now, and don't think in planetary terms or in thousands of years for the health of the Earth itself.

Dogs and cats, though, are not in these wide-sweeping categories. Dogs and cats are breeds created by mankind, for mankind, and are the responsibility of mankind. We have taken away their ability to survive wild, therefore we must make sure they don't have to.

Dogs and cats that have had no choice but to go feral will quickly lose their trust of people. Their immediate offspring will have no appreciation for a kind human hand. Young puppies and kittens are deliberately taught by their parents to distrust people. They go feral at a very young age, soon after their eyes open. They set up feral hierarchies; for instance, one will be designated as *the lookout* while the others eat, if they're fortunate enough to eat. The prospects for survival of the young are poor. Feral cats and dogs often set up housekeeping in abandoned yards, industrial areas, alleys, dumpsters and anywhere they can scrounge for food. There is no one to make sure they're spayed or neutered, so they procreate without control, creating litters of puppies and kittens who inherit a threadbare lifestyle of insect infestations, skin diseases, hunger, misery and frequently terrible death by disease, wounds, or cars, alone.

When you see feral animals, notify the authorities. These animals are better off captured, even if the end result is their being destroyed humanely. Euthanasia in modern science is unfortunate, but peaceful. This is nobody's first choice, but ultimately more decent and less terrorizing than the dismal existence they face on the streets.

If you elect to help these animals personally, or even if you find a cat or dog running wild in your neighborhood that you cannot capture right away, there are ways to help the animal.

Everybody has a basic idea of how to gain the trust of an animal. Obviously, put out food. Even better, put out the food at regular times, then take it away. Get the animal into a habit, so that it equates the food with a particular time of day, and with you, the sound of your car or your door, and let the animal see you as much as possible.

After the animal is used to the food, let him see you more.

Just stand or sit nearby while he eats. Don't approach or reach out. Talk to him. Let him hear your voice. Sitting on the ground or on a low bench is better, because eye-level is less threatening to animals. Be aware this could take a long time, but animals can be quick-minded and will come around to a good thing.

As you gain the animal's trust, you can assess his or her situation. Can you see any infections, injuries, skin patches, red spots, sores? You may be able to consult a vet and slip antibiotics or other medication into the food.

You can also simply provide a wooden box tipped up on its side with some kind of bedding inside. Gradually move the food closer and let the animal get used to the *house*. Once the animal uses the house, put some flea powder on the bedding. Eventually you can translate this into a live trap and capture the pet. Start putting the food near the trap, then eventually inside.

If the pet never becomes accustomed to humans, his future is dim. The best you can do is control the situation. If the animal lives near your house, you may decide to maintain a relationship and let the animal continue to live semi-wild, with a place to sleep somewhere in your yard that is well protected from the weather. When the pet trusts you enough, capture him or her in a live trap, take him or her to the vet, have him neutered, or her spayed, then release him back into the yard. At least he will not contribute to the overpopulation of pets. With your help, he may live an acceptable life.

Feral pets are usually cats, as mentioned before, and while a feral cat's life can be improved some with human participation, the worst thing that can happen is when a feral cat has kittens. Feral kittens are never exposed to human contact. They are born wild—very different from being *born free,* like lions—and quickly become hopelessly wild. At an extremely young age, kittens learn wild habits, learn to stand guard while others eat, for instance, and learn not to trust humans, and it is almost impossible to reverse this.

Kittens learn critical behaviors in their first four weeks, and they need two forces in their lives in order to become balanced pets: they need their cat family, and they need physical human contact. Young kittens should not be separated from their mothers and litter mates before the age of eight weeks. There's a reason for this! Kittens learn discipline, learn their own limitations, and learn playing-without-hurting from their cat mother and litter mates. If separated from them too early, there is a glaring gap in their mental development and in their behavior, probably for life. Kittens too early separated from mom and mates are more likely to be biters, scratchers, or just never to learn how to play without harm. Always leave kittens with their mothers for eight weeks.

If this isn't possible, like, for instance, when we picked up a tiny kitten who had fallen out of a car's wheel well, clearly after a horrific ride from a nearby farm, then you should do all you can to become the kitten's family. You should hold the kitten close to your body as much as possible, teach him that he is secure and that you love him, and play with him with your hand. If you play with your hand, then you can feel when he bites too hard and give him a sharp reprimanding thump. Don't hurt him—just show him that this behavior is wrong. Then you must immediately forgive him. As Cesar Milan says, pets "live in the now." You must never expect your cat or your dog to respond if you hold a grudge. They don't get it.

Back to the feral cat: If there's really nothing you can do, at least call the authorities and alert them to the presence of wild cats and dogs. These animals are always better off in shelters than running wild. They will have care, will not face tragedy under the wheels of a car, by some lingering disease, or by freezing in inclement weather. If they must be destroyed, at least it will be a passive death and not one of lingering misery and terror.

We can't have everything, but we can have better.

Checklist

❑ Be patient and establish a bond with a feral animal by putting out food.

❑ Crouch at eye-level to the animal and watch without approaching.

❑ Put a wooden crate or other shelter outside with flea powder inside.

❑ If you catch the animal, take him or her to a vet for spaying or neutering.

❑ It's usually better to turn a feral animal over to a shelter than let one suffer in the wild. However, many pet rescue organizations stop taking cats periodically because there are so many. Capture, spay or neuter and release if nothing else can be done.

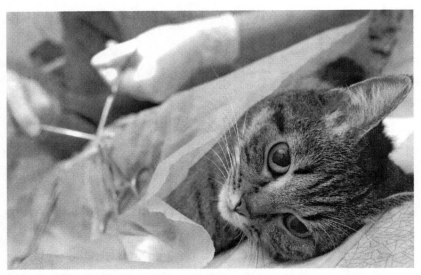

Spay or neuter all cats. It's the only way to cut down a huge problem of overpopulation.

Lesson 28

SPAY, SPAY, SPAY, NEUTER, NEUTER, NEUTER

Thank you, Bob Barker, for saying this every day at the end of *The Price is Right*, and thank you, Drew Carey, for keeping up the tradition. Sadly, there will always be stupid people who do not spay or neuter their pets, resulting in an alarming number of unwanted puppies and kittens. This is an unnecessary tragedy. Spaying or neutering your pet is always less trouble and less expensive than trying to deal with litters of puppies and kittens down the line, and certainly less tragic for the unwanted babies who will probably be given away *free to good homes,* and we know what a joke that is.

There are even heartless fiends who scoop up whole litters of puppies and kittens after they're born and have them destroyed, drown or bury them because it's inconvenient to deal with them in a moral and responsible way. I pity these people's families, for anyone who cannot extend simple compassion to a helpless infant animal will have little for children. I've witnesses this personally in the family of a very close friend. Her husband let his female golden retriever have puppies that he didn't want. He told me, "I put them in a box, took them to the vet, and had them destroyed. What was I supposed to do—raise them?"

Since that day, I have never liked him and have hardly spoken to him. His irresponsibility and cruelty cost him the best friends he could have had—me and my family.

Despite twenty-five years of trying, that family has now broken up because of sheer cold-heartedness. Heartlessness toward animals always shows up in heartlessness toward people. It's part of the same package.

Checklist

❑ Spay.

❑ Neuter.

❑ Spay.

❑ Neuter.

❑ Spay.

❑ Neuter.

Lesson 29

WHEN OTHERS WANT TO DUMP A PET ON YOU

O nce people get the idea you find homes for homeless pets, you may (all right, *will*) find yourself laced with another problem. "I found a dog/cat/iguana. Can I bring it to you?"

This is one of the hardest lessons to learn, and you must learn it: *You are not a drop-off service.*

Once you've trained yourself, you must train your friends and acquaintances. The answer is, "No, you may not, but I'll tell you how to handle the problem yourself. You're perfectly capable of doing it yourself."

You then teach them what you've learned in this book. Or get them a copy, or tell them to get themselves a copy. You tell them to relax, that they won't get stuck, they just have a houseguest for a while. Tell them to clean up the pet, check his health, then find him a home using the advertising technique described here, and charge a dollar figure to cover their expenses. Wish luck and encouragement, offer to check on their progress, but point out clearly that two people who know how to do this is much better than one.

You've spread some good will and take-charge strength to somebody else. Compassion and empowerment are contagious, can be taught, and can be learned.

Yes, I know about farms and country living. Too often people who live in the country become targets for those who want to dump their responsibilities on others. Many farmers or country-dwellers simply let dumped animals live on their property and even feed and shelter them, which is fine, but please spay or neuter the animal and don't allow random breeding. Randomly bred pets in the country are often unsocialized and can't live in homes with people, leading to more breeding and more suffering. If you or someone you know is harboring stray dogs or cats, please go one step further with your kindness and have them fixed.

Or... use this book to recycle them to new homes so there will be room for the next sad case dropped off by the slime of humanity.

When to Take Over

As I said, I don't take over other people's tailed acquisitions. However, there are exceptions. I may take over if the person who has found the pet is somehow infirm and truly unable to handle the situation. An elderly person, for instance, may not be able to handle a rambunctious young stray. That pet will have a better chance with me. It's not my first choice, but may be the best.

There are also other rare situations which have caused me to break my no-handoffs rule. Commonly these are my most heartwarming stories with the happiest endings, because they have such desperate beginnings.

Formerly starved and abandoned at a very young age, little Posie found a wonderful family with a baby daughter for Posie to play with. Here she is with her new "mom."

Posie

Ah, sweet little Posie.

When I was pregnant with my first child, I received a phone call from a young and desperate girl who said she had found a puppy and tried to feed her dog food, but she wouldn't eat. Now, normally my policy had become "I don't take dogs or cats off other people's hands, but I will teach them how to find a new home for their foundling."

Well, we all have to use our judgment and there are no universal rules. This girl sounded desperate and young. The little dog she had found seemed to be in desperate straits that needed an adult's attention, even an adult with very little money and a baby on the way.

The girl showed up with an emaciated female pit bull puppy about six weeks old—too young to be separated from her mother—white with some pale markings, reddened eyes, skeletal body, and zero energy. All the puppy wanted to do was lie down and not get up. The one time I took her outside, she had brief diarrhea, then lay down again. She was dying.

The girl who found her had been trying to feed her dog food. For one thing, this puppy was too young for adult-type dog food, and second, the puppy was dying and was past the point for normal feeding. She refused to eat. Her misery had reached the point at which she had accepted her own death.

The girl, relieved that she had help, left. The puppy was in my hands.

My husband and I didn't have money for additional vet bills, nor the experience to know that this puppy definitely needed real medical intervention with IV fluids and everything an animal hospital could offer her. If the same thing happened today, I would take the puppy to a vet or a shelter, or summon help from the wide community of animal rescue. But in those days, we didn't have the experience or the awareness of where to get help, so we sat on either side of our kitchen table with the dying puppy on the table, on a towel between us.

Since we were about to have a baby in a month or so, we had some baby supplies in the house, including Gerber Baby Oat Meal. I mixed up some of this with a little milk and warmed it up. My husband held the puppy's jaws open and I crammed in some of the oatmeal using a small wooden spoon.

The puppy struggled and tried to fight us. She didn't want food. It was truly a pathetic and pitiful sight. This puppy's previous owners, those who owned her mother, had completely dumped their most basic responsibility, and this puppy was suffering because of them and paying the price for their irresponsibility.

Though the little puppy tried to twist away, we kept pushing little globs of baby oat meal down her gullet. Finally, she had clearly had enough and collapsed. We called it good enough, got a little box and put some towels it in, then laid her in a corner of our soon-to-be-born daughter's bedroom. I slept in that bedroom with the puppy that night. I completely expected to wake in the morning to a dead puppy.

When I got up, I peeked into the box. Lying on her side where we had left her, lay the starved puppy. She rolled her little eye toward me, and her tail began to thump. *Tip, tip, tip, tip.*

I named her Posie. She lay on my lap or on my chest all the time—*all* the time. We kept shoving globs of baby oatmeal into her, then she would collapse on me again. She became my baby. Her body had shut down to a point at which she didn't urinate or defecate. I took her everywhere with me—to visit my parents, to my writers' club, to the breastfeeding.

Gradually, but more quickly than you might think, Posie began raising her head, then began walking unsteadily. She graduated from oatmeal to anything I was eating. I was genuinely her mother: if I was eating a fried egg, she ate some of my egg. If I was eating a PBJ sandwich, she ate some PBJ sandwich. Hamburger, fried chicken, burrito, ice cream—that's how it went for about a week as Posie gained strength and energy—and a round belly!

Our pathetic, starving waif soon morphed into a ball of puppy-energy, racing around after anybody who would play with her, annoying our elegant retriever Sharvan with her silly puppy ways.

During this time we acquired, unwillingly, two other strays. One was a fluffy shepherd-mix puppy five times Posie's size, who came to us with a bad neck wound from a rope that had been too tight. For this we had no choice but the consult a veterinarian, who treated the wound and went easy on the bill. The second stray was a gray tiger kitten we called Needles. Posie, clearly smart and tenacious, ruled the pack.

These three young animals, whom we dubbed The Odd Triple, would play so furiously and scream so loudly that I would lumber into the room and separate them because I thought they were fighting. The kitten would streak away after being freed from the two dogs. Three or four second later, she would race back into the room, all four paws spread on the attack, and the game was on again.

Posie quickly became the roundhouse boss, despite the fact that the other puppy outweighed twice over. I could tease her with a tied-up pantyhose and actually pick her up off the floor as she dangled from it. Her pit-bull stubbornness served her well in these games. By the day she became chubbier, stronger, and happier. When she was done playing, she ran to me, put her little paws up on my leg and asked to be picked up. My role had been defined. I'd scoop her up, she would curl into a ball on top of my big pregnant tummy, sigh heavily, and immediately fall asleep. I was her mommy-pillow.

We found homes for all three of the Odd Triple. Posie went to live with our then-mail carrier and his wife and their baby girl. Several weeks later, I phoned to check on Posie, who will always be one of the favorites among our foundlings. She was doing fine, as the lady of the house happily declared. We went to visit, and saw Posie's favorite activity: dragging the baby around in the wheelie chair, with the baby laughing wildly.

Posie's new mom said we would have to get together for a pizza some time.

"You won't leave Posie at home, will you?" I asked.

"What?" she protested. "Our other daughter? Never!"

Posie remains one of our best stories, one that involved hope and luck and instinct and all the other things that make up for inexperience and lack of money. As mentioned, today I would do things differently because now I understand how much better

Posie's chances would have been with a veterinarian on her side. She could easily have died, but we got lucky and she was just at the brink when she could be brought back from death's door.

That's my little Posie—my baby when I needed a baby, and I her mommy when she needed a mommy.

Checklist

❏ Be firm. You are not a drop-off point.

❏ Coach others with strays; be a resource but not a dumping ground.

❏ Make exceptions only in rare cases when some is incapable of helping a stray.

❏ Tell yourself, and others, to relax. Keeping the stray is temporary.

Lesson 30

The Return Policy

This is the hard part, the part that tests your commitment to do as well as you possibly can on this Earth for these stray pets. What a victory to be rid of a troublesome houseguest! You can relax, clean up, sleep well, and feel great knowing you saved a life and connected a doomed pet with a chance for a good future.

A few moments in fantasyland. Ahhhh...

Now, wake up. Robert Burns was right when he said the best-laid plans of mice and men—and dogs and cats and good Samaritans—often go awry. Not everything works out as we would dream or assume. I gave a kitten to a charming elderly lady who seemed just right and apparently knew what she was getting into. Three days later she called to return my kitten. Raising a young animal was too much for a senior lady. She would've been perfect for an older pet, many of whom unfortunately also need homes. I took my kitten back and recommended that she consult the Humane Society for an old cat, already settled and trained, because there are way too many adult animals out there who have a very hard time finding homes. She thanked me and thought that was actually a good idea for her situation. I hope she followed through.

Notice I said *my kitten*. All the waifs I find are *mine* in my mind. With this idea firmly grounded, I do a better job finding homes and embrace the responsibility for a successful outcome in the long run. Success in the short run is only half the job. If the home doesn't last until the end of the pet's longest possible life, then you haven't succeeded. After a few clumsy years of not knowing what really became of my little foundlings, I started making phone calls after a couple weeks or months to check on them. The story was almost always good, give or take circumstances like Kisha, in which I will never know the true outcome and will always be haunted. For people like us, out of sight is definitely not out of mind. Accept that.

If I had been as experienced then as I am now, the story would have turned out very differently. I now have an ironclad return policy. Anyone who adopts a pet from me can return that pet within a certain reasonable time period, usually a couple of months. I retain the right to call and check on my pets, and hopefully the chance to visit.

This has turned out to be an excellent barometer for whether or not my stray is going to the best home possible. If potential owners balk at the idea of giving me phone rights or visitation possibilities, I think twice about sending my pet with them. *They've already seen my home—why can't I see theirs?*

Return of adopted pets doesn't happen often, but it does happen. It's always inconvenient. Accept that it will be. Accept also that for your inconvenience, for the trouble of going through the housing and adoption process all over again, you will have more experience and personal strength for the next time, that you've fulfilled every last bit of your moral commitment and done what's right, and you will also know for certain that your waif is getting an even better third chance than his second chance. A stray who gets three chances is truly blessed. You are the blessing.

Explain this *strongly* to anyone who adopts a pet from you. Explain that you will check on the pet's progress after two weeks, then do it. Explain that you even reserve the right to drop in and see the pet later. It's not legally defensible, but at least this puts your adopters on notice that you're serious, and if they don't want you to come over, then they shouldn't adopt your pet. And you shouldn't let them.

Explain that the *Return Policy* works in their favor also; if things don't work out, you would rather the pet be returned to you than passed along or dropped off into some unknown situation. They'll sleep better, and so will you.

The Return Policy is its own reward. You'll be at peace with yourself, and that alone is well worth the extra trouble.

Checklist

❏ Set a return policy time frame of about two months.

❏ Insist on the right to check up on the pet.

❏ Don't allow someone to adopt a pet unless he or she agrees to allow you to visit the new home.

Young wild animals sometimes need human intervention to survive.
Make sure it's obvious that they need help. Otherwise, leave them
alone.

Lesson 31

The Occasional Bird

I don't have many wild bird stories, but I'll offer you what I know.

Generally, I don't recommend that you touch or capture wild birds or any wild animal species. Animals in the wild can carry many types of diseases and vermin. For your sake and theirs, they are better off being left alone unless the situation is obviously dire for them, like an owl caught in a wire fence. Even injured wild animals usually shouldn't be approached by anyone other than trained animal handlers. Wild animals are not accustomed to being approached; in the wild, injured animals are only approached by other animals who want to eat them. If a human approaches, a wild animal thinks the same thing—that you want to eat them. They will fight back. In those cases, I recommend calling the authorities, 911, local law enforcement, or professional animal handlers.

That being said, I've found myself faced with wild birds in distress a few times and have had to intervene.

The Great White Hunter

The Spook, our cat, otherwise known as Sabertooth the Great White Hunter, is a ruthless predatory feline who, when she was young, frequently caught birds despite the jingle of her collar and tag. She is a wonderful breed of cat for personality and companionship: an American short-haired white. Our first cat, Simmony, was the same breed or type. The American short-haired white may not be an actual breed, but just a type of cat, but so far with our two household pals the results have been terrific. Like Simmony, they sometimes come with a blue eye and a yellow eye, and are sometimes deaf, though neither Simmony nor the Spook had that problem. Spooky's eyes are green.

I've avoided putting bird attractors such as seeding flowers, birdseed, birdhouses or birdbaths in my yard, but there's only so much to be done. Studies have proven that belling or tagging cats really makes no difference in their hunting abilities. They learn to deal with the equipment. Your only really effective option is either to keep your cat indoors all the time, which I elect not to do, or to let your cat out later in the day, after wild birds have done most of their feeding.

Nature takes its course, and we must accept that most of the time. Cats are predators and birds are prey. This order has been set up for eons.

Twice, Spooky dragged sizable birds, still alive, through her cat door. One was a female robin, quite roughed up and shocky, tucked in a window sill when I found her on the enclosed porch.

I put on a glove—don't touch wild birds with your bare hands if you can avoid it—and slowly closed in. With a quick motion I managed to grab this bird. Nothing appeared to be bleeding or broken, so I took the bird outside and placed it in a hanging basket on our sittin'-under tree. We sat back and watched as she took a nap. A while later I thought she might be too far gone and reached to check, at which point she launched and winged into the big trees.

Spooky was annoyed, but forgave me later.

Another bird was less fortunate. My daughter came home to find a blizzard of gray-white feathers carpeting the porch—but no dead bird. There's no such thing as feathers without a bird.

And there it was—in the windowsill—a ravaged dove. Spooky had really chewed up this poor bird. Most of its back was bare and bleeding.

I choose to let Spook be an indoor-outdoor cat because we live in a fairly good neighborhood for such a life, and I believe a cat's life is far richer, healthier and better adjusted if the cat can do what cats naturally do—run and roam and hunt and play. I understand there are other philosophies, but each of us must make decisions right for ourselves. If a cat is tagged or phone-numbered and there is a limited danger of busy roads nearby, there is little reason he or she shouldn't enjoy the fullness of a life with some interest and diversity in it. Cats and dogs have intelligent minds which need stimulation. They suffer from debilitating boredom if stuck inside or tied to one spot all the time, just as people tend to suffer from lack of stimulation. We all know that being a shut-in is a gloomy sentence for anyone who isn't a reptile.

But she *is* mine, and what she does is my responsibility. For the dove, I called our vet, who offered to look at the wounded bird. If the bird was too injured, the vet would euthanize it for five dollars. I caught the poor terrified bird in a box and took it in. The vet pointed out some serious damage and we put the bird out of its misery, thus sparing it either death by injury or by further cat torture.

Animals can't make these choices. It's up to us.

The Duckling

One very tiny happy ending occurred while we attended a friend's outdoor wedding in Fenton, Michigan, at a riverside gazebo near a spillway. There are wild ducks in that river, and as we waited for the photographing to wrap up, I noticed a baby duck caught in the spillway current and being carried rapidly toward the wooded area downriver, on the wrong side of the dam from its mother and siblings. It had been caught by the current and couldn't possibly paddle back. The tiny waif was peeping madly. What a pitiful sight. Before long I had several people following me into the woods, all of us dressed for a formal evening.

The baby duck ended up stuck on the rocks at the riverside, well into the wooded area, with no hope of finding its way back to its mother. Off with the dancing shoes. I stuck one foot into the cold water, only to be outpaced by a teenaged girl who went in up to her ankles, crossed the river, and scooped up the panicking duckling.

I offered to take the duckling, but this girl proved to be more experienced. She lived on a farm with barnyard fowl and ducks. If she couldn't return the baby to its own mother, she would take it back to her farm.

Happy ending. There's always one possible; we just have to grab hold of the problem and hunt around for the happy ending.

Most wild animals are best left alone. Nature has a course to take and generally we are safer not interfering. But I do advocate interfering when situations are as clear-cut as with the duckling in the spillway.

The Bird in the Basement

One day my mother called from her house, which at the time was a large tri-level with a big basement. There was a bird in her basement. She had called the authorities, who advised her to "just let nature take its course." In other words, she should just wait until the poor panicked bird died of dehydration and starvation. Well, this didn't sit well. My son Gordon and I grabbed a butterfly net which I'd purchased at a dollar store, my emergency bird cage, some work gloves, and off we went, to the rescue.

When we reached my mother's house, there was a frantic blue jay rushing about in her big fir trees, calling and calling. It was a male, the mate of the unfortunate bird trapped in the basement.

The bird in the basement was in a complete panic, flying erratically around, slamming into walls and cupboards and trying to get out the one small window, which of course was closed. We had no idea how the bird could possibly have gotten inside the basement, but there she was. Gordon went after the bird with the butterfly net, and after several minutes of stalking managed to capture the bird up against the window. With the work gloves on, I took hold of the bird, net and all. She was frantic, but exhausted enough that I could take her out of the net and carry her upstairs. After a brief introduction to my mom, who was very glad to see this bird in my hands, we went outside and made a short ceremony of setting her free. She flew into the fir trees and joined her confused and relieved mate. Another happy ending.

Birdie in the Window

While visiting my husband's mother at the family cottage out in the twigs in the middle of Michigan, my sister-in-law Katherine and I were chatting when something hit the big picture window. Katherine went to the window, looked down and gasped. There was a little bird, about the size of a sparrow, unconscious on the sandy ground. We went out to check, and the little bird was alive but stunned and breathing heavily. With gloves on, Katherine picked it up. We discovered that it had a weird white globby substance stuck between its upper and lower beaks, something like half-dried glue or chewing gum. The poor thing was probably in a complete panic to free its mouth from the glob, and, frantic, had hit the window.

I tried to pull the gummy glob out of its mouth, but the glob was sticky and the beak pulled forward rather than releasing the white gluey thing. I finally broke my own rule and took the gloves off, so I could get a better grip on the circumstance. While holding the tiny beak instead of just holding the bird's head, I was able to pull out the glob. I never did find out what the substance was, but it came out cleanly, to our relief.

We dripped some water into the bird's mouth, in case it was dehydrated. After that, other than calling a vet, there wasn't much we could do. We put the bird in a box on a soft cloth and put it outside to come out of its state of shock.

That didn't sit well either. Any predator could come and find the bird, served up in its box. We took the bird out of the box and settled in it a crook of sturdy branches on a large bush, a more natural and camouflaged environment, and checked on it from time to time, without approaching it too closely. It had certainly had enough shocks for one day.

Sure enough, after about an hour the bird suddenly launched and flew away.

Another good save—because a couple of animal-lovers happened to see the fall of a single sparrow.

Wild Things

Sick or injured birds, squirrels, raccoons, possums, snakes, rats and other wild creatures are not my area of experience. If they are also not yours, you are better off keeping your distance. These animals can be dangerous or diseased and need experienced handlers. I was scratched very badly once by someone's pet rabbit. Even animals that seem passive, like white-tailed deer or rabbits, can pack a vicious kick, bite or scratch, and an adult deer can kill a human. Owls and other large birds are hunters and can inflict ghastly wounds. They have the equipment to survive in the wilderness, and you are an enemy in their eyes.

An injured or trapped wild animal is dangerous. If a situation warrants intervention, call an agency or company which specializes in dealing with wild rescues or pest problems. When dealing with any animal you don't know, even dogs and cats, you must always consider your own safety first. However, in the days of cell phones and instant communication, you can contact those who are better equipped to deal with such problems.

When your tendency to rescue animals is toward wild animals, you have two other options. One, of course, is to learn how to handle wild animals before a dire situation arises. Many people learn to deal with animals which tend to need help in their individual areas, for instance if you live in an area which leaves baby rabbits in your back yard from time to time, or an area where barn owls turn up in need now and then. Most often, baby animals that appear abandoned are not actually abandoned, but simply waiting for a parent to return. Learn the traits of truly abandoned or endangered baby animals. Your local wildlife refuge or humane organization can put you on the trail to people who know what to do and will teach you.

Second, for the more adventurous among us, there's almost no limit. You may find yourself drawn to birds of prey, bats, songbirds, deer, or other non-domesticated animals, and wish to establish a recovery area on your property. There are apprenticeships and licensing requirements for those who rehabilitate exotic animals, refugees from zoos or animals from the wild. How far your take this wish to help animals is entirely up to you and your personal resources and energy.

The key is this: *Others have already done this. Learn from them.* Volunteer at a wild animal refuge or a zoo. Do not plunge in without considerable consideration, experience and training, and even then, be sure that you always respect and fear any wild breed of animal. Don't get overconfident. That leads to maulings.

Do it right, do it safely, build a support system, and support others.

Checklist

❑ Find local rescue groups for wild animals.

❑ Log phone numbers into your cell.

❑ If you're going to help birds have a small cage on hand.

❑ Handle them with work gloves.

❑ Have a butterfly net.

❑ Volunteer at zoos or refuges to work with exotic animals.

❑ Consider your own safety first.

❑ If you have an outdoor cat, don't have a bird attractor or feeder.

Lesson 32

Keep a Scrapbook

Take a photo of each foundling, then one of the pet with his new family. Record the dates, circumstances, your thoughts and little memories about the discovery and adoption of this pet. Record the name, address and phone number of the new family and let them see you writing the information down. If they will give you a driver's license number, take it; you'll never use it, but the taking gives people a sense that you're serious about finding a good home for this pet. People can be psychologically urged to do a better job with their new commitment by these little gestures.

Make a calendar, and do bother to make that follow-up phone call in two weeks, then again in another month. These calls can be nerve-wracking to make, but usually the result is an enthusiastic happy ending. The adoptive family is usually please to tell you how well your friend is doing, and if things are not going so well, you can offer then and there to come pick up the pet. At least you will know.

With your scrapbook, you'll have a pleasant record to show around, for your own sense of accomplishment and to inspire others.

Chessie

My husband and I were prowling a local freight train yard for research and photographs for a writing project. On the way home, we spotted a gangly Lab-mix puppy with a ratty rope around her neck, frantically sniffing around an abandoned gas station. My instincts, well-honed by now, went off like an alarm.

We pulled over. I stepped out of the car, knelt down, and whistled once.

The rangy black dog perked up instantly, looked around, spotted me, and rushed to me—but she didn't stop when she got to me. She continued to climb up my legs, up my chest, and locked her long skinny forelegs around my neck. She tucked her head under my ear, pressed her chin to my shoulder, and hugged me like a child all the way back. I never even saw her face until we got home.

We called her Chessie, after the Chesapeake and Ohio train yard we had just left. Chessie was a prime example of the idea that dogs and cats are intelligent, loving creatures that have emotion and devotion just as people do. She was completely devoted to me, for she saw me as her savior. She understood she had been alone, abandoned, helpless, and now she wasn't anymore. She absolutely knew.

This is often the case with adopted pets. Dundee, our big red dopey setter who came to live with us after Sharvan died, has never forgotten Tony and Wendy, the people who rescued him when he was one day from euthanasia at the Humane Society. Though they visit very rarely, he knows exactly who they are and will actually climb into their laps.

Dogs and cats know when they have been saved. Chessie

certainly understood, to a degree that the people who came to adopt her were reluctant to take her away from me. She clearlyadored me as her hero in life. I explained to them that Chessie indeed loved me and I loved her, but I had to pass her along to a new loving family so there would be room for the next one who needed my help.

The situation worked out beautifully. Chessie grew up into a lovely, delicate-faced housedog that was the gem of her family. I went on to save many more pets, because I had the room to do so.

Who needs fiction when reality can be this rewarding?

Checklist

❏ Take photos of each pet you save.

❏ Keep records of their new owners and check in with them periodically.

❏ Keep a scrapbook for yourself; it'll be a source of accomplishment and inspiraton.

Lesson 33

A Quantum Leap In Animal Rescue

Petfinder.com

It's a new world from when I started picking up strays. In those days I was ignorant and alone, unaware of other help that might be available to me. There were county animal control departments and there was the Humane Society, but not much else. I had no way to *network,* as we say now, with others interested in animal rescue or to get help when I needed it.

Today, the level of awareness is rising very fast, and we are all connected. There are multiple animal rescue groups, many specific to size, breed, mutts, cats, and they're easy to find. On TV we have wonderful and successful shows like *Animal Cops* that showcase the ghastly truths about neglect and cruelty to animals, ramp up the public's awareness that these things are not only horrible but illegal, and give attention and honor to the people who put themselves on the line to rescue the helpless victims. From those of us in the animal rescue world, I'd like to offer my deepest thanks and respect to all the heroes who

This is Honey, an American bulldog rescued by Diane's brother, Lance Carey.

engage in animal rescue both for a living and not. It is not always the most pleasant of lifestyles, but it's desperately needed and we also need to spread out to other nations in the world where animals are tragically abused and neglected.

Technology has given a wondrous gift to the world of animal rescue and relocation. In past, when someone wanted a dog or cat, the resources were limited to newspaper ads, word of mouth, and personal visits to shelters. The result was that many people chose the wrong breed for their lifestyles or made snap decisions, and many animals ended up abandoned, surrendered, stray or otherwise cast away after the situation failed to work out. While the animal population is at crisis levels, it's now easier than ever to select the right dog or cat for your personal lifestyle, and to have a successful lifelong match with that pet. The number of animals euthanized every year is declining. Thank goodness! Thank the goodness of all the people who work to mitigate this appalling problem.

Matching breed traits, personality, size, age and temperament to the right household is critical, as we've discussed. Luckily, with the Internet, it's now also very easy. A person in search of an animal companion can shop for and virtually dial-a-pet, using a computer search process called *Petfinder.com.*

Petfinder.com was started by a married couple who pooled their interests—animals and computers—to start this wonderful website. The site links thousands of rescue and shelter operations, who advertise their adoptable pets. The simple, user-friendly format allows you to click on which type of animal you want to find, then pick breed, size, age, gender, and general location, so you can find adoptable pets near your zip code.

If you select, for instance, *dog,* then the breed *Irish setter,* size *large,* Petfinder.com will take you to all the choices matching your criteria, available within driving distance, along with photos of most pets, their temporary names, age, location and gender. When you click on a particular pet, you will get that pet's history and temperament, usually written by the foster parent, the person with whom the pet has been living or the shelter operators.

When you need help

If you scroll down on Petfinder.com's homepage, you'll find an *animal welfare group search.* You put your zip code in, and the engine takes you to animal rescue and shelter operations near you. This connects you to people who can help you in almost any capacity of rescuing animals, including those who are better set up to foster a particular pet. If you're going on vacation or are physically infirm, or have other limitations, these people will find a recourse that can take the pet off your hands. Be prepared to make a donation to the rescue, so your pet is not just another burden. A $50-$100 donation, or more if you can afford it, is a big boost in paying for food and care. Most animal rescue people are not wealthy, and pets take money, food, vet care and time. It is money well spent.

You can also search for a rescue operation by breed. This can be a quick way to recycle a pet into the rescue system.

Sergei's story

A puppy named Sergei was another example of a family's choosing the wrong breed and wrong everything else. This family had almost no front yard and no back yard at all, yet adopted a Lab-Rottweiler mixed puppy. They had several children in this second-marriage situation, so the quiet and small-boned mother had her hands full just with the kids. They did the dumbest thing they could do: adopt an untrained dog. Of course, they needed one more responsibility! Busy families don't need one more thing. Just don't get a dog.

The mother had no time to give Sergei the walks he needed to use up his puppy energy. She also did not have the intestinal fortitude to insist that the kids walk the dog as part of their responsibility in the home. She didn't know how to train a dog, so Sergei had many accidents in the house. Eventually they gave up on him.

Sadly, they didn't bother to find him a better, more qualified home. They just stuck him in fenced area behind the house, an area no larger than a dining room table. And there he stayed, hearing his family inside the house, seeing people pass on the street, barking helplessly and desperately for attention, disturbing the neighbors. He was pretty much ignored from then on.

One day I finally had enough and knocked on the door to talk to the wife. I pointed out that Sergei was virtually being tortured back there, ignored, friendless, seeing the world pass him by every minute. She agreed. I offered to take Sergei and find him a better home, because clearly these dopes were never going to do it. If they got rid of Sergei, it would be to the pound, where he would likely be euthanized.

She said she would talk to her husband.

The next day, while outside chatting with a friend who lived near Sergei's house, a man stalked across the intersection from that house. It was the husband. I expected a conversation about Sergei and was ready for it, but he wasn't in a talking mood. In front of my eighty five-year-old friend, the man began cursing me out and demanding that I mind my own business. He shouted at me with foul language and declared that his dog was "just fine" in the tiny backyard pen.

I tried to speak, to point out that dogs are pack animals that need to be with their families, that become neurotic and unbalanced if they're left alone, that he was being unfair to his pet and that I could help.

He pushed closer to me. I didn't back off.

He shouted louder, "My dog gets food and he gets water!"

Okay, two can play at this game.

Matching his tone, I shouted, "Food, water and ignored!"

He shouted something else and stalked back to his house. My elderly friend was astonished. "Is that the father of all those children?" she asked in a mournful way. Clearly this man was as bad a father as he was a pet owner. After all, the way we treat our pets is never far off the way we treat the people around us.

We sadly watched this crass fool disappear into his house. The screen door clapped shut. There was nothing we could do for the children or for Sergei.

Meanwhile, Sergei barked desperately for attention,

disturbing the neighborhood, while every day hearing the voices of his family inside the house from which he had been banned. It was not Sergei's fault, but the fault of his owners.

One day almost a year later, the wife showed up on my front step in tears. She told me that she was leaving her husband and taking the child that was hers with her. Her husband, she said, had to learn that he couldn't treat women "the way he does." If I still wanted to rescue her dog, I would have to take him right now.

I said, "Go get him."

She brought Sergei to me immediately. Confused, Sergei huddled in a corner on my porch while I contemplated what had just happened. I feared the abusive husband would return and try to reclaim the dog he had thoroughly ignored, and I would have no legal recourse other than to give him his dog. My only recourse was to get Sergei out of my house that afternoon.

Using Petfinder, I instantly found a shelter which handled Rottweilers in my general area. I made one phone call, explained the situation, and a young lady who ran foster care and adoption out of her cottage, on a small lake about an hour and a half from me, offered to take Sergei. I drove him to her that day, eliminating the chance of his returning to his nightmare situation down the block.

The last time I checked on Sergei, he had been renamed Buddy and enjoyed chasing balls and playing in the lake. His future would be good from now on.

The last I heard about the family down the block, the mother had returned under certain conditions, hopefully that the father would no longer abuse her, the children or any pets they were dumb enough to get in the future. *Hopefully.* While this is one of my most satisfying rescues, I think often of the children in that household, and of all the children in abusive situations, and the helpless pets given by fate to people like that. I don't feel sorry for the women; they are adults and should get out and report the very first sign of abuse by any man. No woman has to live that way.

But the kids and the pets do. They have no choice.

If you know of an abusive situation, don't be afraid to speak up. Interfere. It's not "none of your business." Abuse and neglect of children and animals are everybody's business. At least the victims will hear that someone thinks the situation is wrong. Sometimes that's enough to change everything.

The rescue system stands ready to help you as you reach out to animals who are in desperate need of intervention. While it's better if you learn to move pets to the right homes yourself, certainly a pet is better off cycled into the foster care/rescue system than left without aid or comfort.

Take a tour on Petfinder.com; learn to use it, become familiar with shelters around you, and you will become part of the world that matches pets to the right people, for successful *forever* homes.

Checklist

❏ Familiarize yourself with Petfinder.com.

❏ Make a financial contribution to shelters and rescue in the Petfinder network.

❏ Be aggressive when you see a pet being abused your neglected. Interfere. It *is* your business.

Lesson 34

Finding Your Own Ideal Pet

Cairo's Story

If you're looking for a dog and have not decided on a breed, a good first step is to watch a dog show like the Westminster or AKC dog competitions. You'll see all the pure breeds, and get a first impression of what you like. Also, pets you've owned in the past, if any, will give you a clue as to what worked and what didn't. I like setters, and thus was able to find my wonderful Cairo by searching for Irish and Gordon setters on the Internet. He was living in a shelter in Indiana, unwanted for a year and a half—his whole life. He's the dog of my dreams—and I've had two dogs-of-my-dreams before him: Sharvan, who died at eleven of cancer, and Dundee, who passed away after a long life of fifteen years. Sharvan, we now know, was a flat-coated retriever, one of a charming and adorable breed who remain active and puppy-like all their lives, love children, and make great family pets. As long as the owner understands that the dog is at risk for cancer, you can have a marvelous decade or

Cairo, a Gordon setter, or a "cross between Zorro and Big Bird." At this writing he is 12 years old, runs every day, and is a 90-pound lap dog.

so with a flat-coat. They're also gaining in popularity and have been taking awards at dog shows, recognized as great field dogs and even greater family pets. Flat-coats are good hunters, but I strongly recommend that no one gets a flat-coat to leave outside in the kennel. They are warm-hearted, people-oriented dogs and need to be in the house with their families, not locked outside until hunting season. That goes for all dogs, but especially for the setter-retriever breeds, which suffer terrible stress and loneliness when separated from people.

Having been through the cancer problem once, I didn't want to experience it again. Therefore, I knew I didn't want another flat-coat, or at least wanted a mix. Mixed breeds can solve many problems; many purebreds come with endemic health troubles and personality quirks which are well watered-down by mixing. You can still get the traits and "look" you like, without negative inbred aspects.

For the first time in my life, I was able to "pick" a dog. My other dogs had come to me through happenstance. This was my first chance to think about what I wanted and take the time to look for it. I used *Petfinder.com* to look for an Irish setter or Gordon setter, large, and young--because I wanted my children to experience a young dog.I was actually looking for a female puppy, but took a chance on a 1½ year-old male that was listed as a black Irish setter by a shelter called Mixed Up Mutts in La Porte, Indiana (email: *info@mixedupmutts.com*).

Mixed Up Mutts specializes in mixed-breed dogs and cats, because mutts often have trouble finding homes. This is an irony because mutts are very often the best of dogs—excellent personalities, good temperament, fewer health problems than purebreds.

I asked for a few more photos, which MUM sent right away. With my elder son, Gordon Brodeur, we drove halfway and the MUM folks drove the other half. We met in the middle.

Out of their van tumbled this gangly and extremely tall cross between Zorro and Big Bird. He was eighteen months old and housebroken, but otherwise not well-trained. After getting used to his surprising height, we fell in love with the goofy, lanky, friendly Gordon setter, probably mixed, but still looking very much like a Gordon setter. He was huge, hairy, hilarious, big-eyed, ill-mannered and instantly adorable. Setters are like that—they remain puppies for most of their lives.

We took Big Bird home, wrangled for a while about what to name him, and settled on Cairo.

Cairo is black with white markings, but is really double-dark brown. With the sun behind him, he looks like a black dog in red smoke. I gave him a "show cut," which means his head and back are shaved, but his long silky hair flows from the flanks, tail, and down the backs of the legs, like a dog-show Gordon setter. He suddenly looked less goofy and much more elegant, and I've received many compliments on his handsomeness over the years. If only the viewers knew he's also neurotic, silly, clingy, needy, cuddly and always in the way! And afraid of thunder. He turns into a giant chicken if it rains.

I spent about a year training him regularly and consistently, and bringing his manners to a polite level. He no longer runs off, does not need a leash, and has turned into a ninety-pound lap dog. Now I'll have a perfect, loving and well-integrated pet for, I hope, a good long time. Cross your fingers for me, because I can no longer imagine life without my Cairo. Petfinder.com and Mixed Up Mutts, thank you!

A good option before you shop is to scan Petfinder.com's list of over 200 breeds. The idea that purebreds or fancy breeds can only be acquired through breeders is ludicrous and counterproductive. Everyone who wants a dog or cat should consider shelters first, not breeders or pet stores, the latter of which often get puppies and kittens from puppy mills. Spend a few evenings watching *Animal Cops, Animal Precinct* or *Pet Patrol* on TV, then tell me the world needs more animals to be bred. I advocate a moratorium on breeding dogs and cats for about twenty years, until the voluminous overpopulation of unwanted pets is relieved. Yes, twenty years. We simply have too many dogs and cats in the world and every puppy or kitten born, no matter how pedigreed, is an added burden and leaves another pet without a home. One needs only tour the Petfinder listings to gain a sense of how desperate the problem is: shelters are overloaded, foster parents often house several dogs or cats at a time, and the sad stories are unending. Look at the numbers beside the listing of breeds: that number represents all the unwanted pets just in your immediate region. Multiply that by the whole country, the continent, the world, and you begin to realize the true scope of this unnecessary tragedy. These are good dogs, good cats, and they deserve homes as much as any highly priced animal. There's no doubt that some of them *were* highly priced at one time, but have fallen out of "value" in all but the hearts of the decent human beings who care for them and who adopt them. There is no amount of money high enough to get Cairo away from me; his worth is beyond pedigrees, trophies or awards. Who really cares in the long run?

Adoption Fees at Shelters

Reputable shelters and foster care providers require that pets be spayed or neutered, usually before they are given a home. When you pay an adoption fee, that fee covers medical care, neutering, shots and other bare-bones handling needs, so don't flinch at paying a fair one. In the short and long run, the adoption fee is a modest donation you'll have to bear anyway if you were to take the pet to the vet for these services. The fee also helps keep the shelters running, providing food and care for unwanted pets during their holding periods. Many of these pets are in foster care, living in real homes with people who are working on improving the pets' habits, housebreaking, socialization, and so on. Your chances of getting a pretty well-adjusted pet are quite good.

Those pets which are in animal control facilities and other humane organizations are often living their lives in cages and are in even more dire need of homes, though they will probably take a little extra effort to housebreak and socialize. If foster care can do it, so can you. Don't shy away from adopting a pet living in a kennel situation; just be aware that time, patience, and method are needed to make an adjustment and provide training. Don't be frustrated too soon, and ask for help and advice from the shelter. Dogs often take up to a year to really settle down into a household routine, so don't expect instant perfection. There is always a growing period.

Shelters, and especially foster parents, are fussy about the people to whom they give their pets. We are all well aware of the fact that our homeless pets have been through rough times with emotional and physical distress, and that their second chance is probably their last. We go for the best match, even if it takes time. We will ask many questions. Answer all the questions honestly. It's not a job application. You want a good, true match. Don't take offense if they are strict or even cynical. They're out for the pet's welfare, and in the end, that's better all around.

As you focus on a dog or cat, you'll have to move along with dispatch. While some pets are in rescue literally for years, others can move quickly. Make a considered decision, but be prepared to make a fairly quick one. Make arrangements for the pet to be returned to the original shelter if the match doesn't work. Most shelters allow this and even prefer it.

Be prepared for a background check. They'll want to know about your pets in the past and what happened to them. They'll want to contact your vet to see how well you maintain your pets' medical needs. They'll want a few references who know about your household. Be assured—this is the good side of nosiness! Don't be insulted or annoyed. These questions are for the best.

Checklist

- ❏ If you're interested in a specific breed, do your homework. Watch a dog show on TV.

- ❏ Mutts may be a better choice; check out Mixed Up Mutts and Petfinder.comon the Internet.

- ❏ Shelters are great resources to find a pet and to learn about them. Visit and ask questions.

Lesson 35

What Rescuing a Stray Does for You

You've decided to be aggressive when you see roaming dogs and cats. Though this seems completely selfless, it is in fact a self-strengthening choice of growth and empowerment. Yes, there is tremendous inconvenience and sometimes heartache. You must accept that; when you do, the downs actually get easier. You get better with planning and experience, and before long the trouble, strife, inconveniences and frustrations begin to shrink.

I was confused and intimidated the first few times I picked up strays. Now, I'm the person who takes charge. I don't even look for other people to do it anymore. Once I even argued with another person over who was better qualified to seize control of a wandering hound. I won.

Picking up stray, helpless, abandoned pets gives a human being surprising self-confidence. Since learning to seize control of these kinds of situations, I've gone one step further and taken first aid and CPR courses. Now I stop at car accidents and jump in to help.

I no longer waffle about troublesome problems. Decisions come easier, solutions faster. I don't wait for "someone else" to act. I've set broken bones, calmed people in shock and handled diabetic emergencies.

I also have the pleasure of knowing I've inspired other people to pick up and help strays, including my own children, my mother, and several friends, some of whom have become even more aggressive than I am. I've sponsored children in Third World countries, and in 1994 adopted a baby boy from Guatemala, our son Ben, mostly because of confidence in myself forged by a take-charge can-do attitude.

All this from picking up scruffy dogs and cats wandering the open streets?

You bet!

Go thou, and do likewise!

There's nothing like a happy ending!

RESOURCES

This is not meant to be a comprehensive list, but just to give you starting points. You will soon find that there is a huge network of animal welfare interests in the world and that you are not alone!

THE INTERNET

GOOGLE

Search by phrase, breed, rescue, kennels, training needs, coupons, health needs, veterinarians, animal welfare advocacy, expert pet care, abuse or neglect issues, therapy animal programs, charities, laws, political activity, conferences, or any other interest you have.

Connect with people in the rescue community; get advice, help, information, or just camaraderie.

Find your local humane organization, in the United States and Canada, or all over the world.

Find organizations to which you can donate money, time, or talent.

PETFINDER.COM:

Find rescue groups, humane organizations, animal welfare advocates, and shelters in any geographic area.

Find rescue organizations by specific breeds or types of pets, such as dog or cat breeds, birds, rabbits, horses, barnyard animals, and exotic pets.

SHELTERS AND HUMANE ORGANIZATIONS

Human Society of the United States

American Society for the Prevention of Cruelty to Animals (ASPCA)

American Humane Society

International Association of Human-Animal Interaction Organizations (IAHAIO)

ANIMAL TV SHOWS

Animal Cops, Animal Precinct; The Dog Whisperer; Animal Planet; Call of the Wildman; The National Geographic Channel; It's Me Or The Dog; Animal Miracles; Dogs With Jobs; My Cat From Hell. Eukanuba and the American Kennel Club stage dog shows and competitions